# 500

## *Tips*

*for*

## *Open and*

## *Flexible Learning*

**500 Tips from Kogan Page**

*500 Computing Tips for Teachers and Lecturers,* Phil Race and Steve McDowell
*500 Tips for EFL Teachers,* Maggy NcNorton and Phil Race
*500 Tips for Further and Continuing Education Lecturers,* David Anderson, Sally Brown and Phil Race
*500 Tips for Getting Published: a guide for educators, researchers and professionals,* Dolores Black, Sally Brown, Abby Day and Phil Race
*500 Tips for Primary Teachers,* Emma Packard, Nick Packard and Sally Brown
*500 Tips for Quality Enhancement in Universities and Colleges,* Sally Brown, Phil Race and Brenda Smith
*500 Tips for Research Students,* Sally Brown, Liz McDowell and Phil Race
*500 Tips for School Improvement,* Helen Horne and Sally Brown
*500 Tips for Teachers,* Sally Brown, Carolyn Earlam and Phil Race
*500 Tips for Trainers,* Phil Race and Brenda Smith
*500 Tips for Tutors,* Phil Race and Sally Brown
*500 Tips on Assessment,* Sally Brown, Phil Race and Brenda Smith

# 500

# *Tips*

# *for*
# *Open and*
# *Flexible Learning*

PHIL RACE

**KOGAN**
**PAGE**

London • Sterling (USA)

First published in 1998

Kogan Page Limited
120 Pentonville Road
London N1 9JN, UK
and
Stylus Publishing Inc.
22883 Quicksilver Drive
Sterling, VA 20166, USA

**British Library Cataloguing in Publication Data**

A CIP record for this book is available from the British Library.

ISBN 0 7494 2410 9

Typeset by Jo Brereton, Primary Focus, Haslington, Cheshire
Printed and bound in the UK, Biddles Ltd, Guildford and Kings Lynn

# Contents

Acknowledgements     **vii**
Introduction     **1**

**Chapter 1    Terminology, contexts, benefits**     **5**
1   What sorts of learning?     7
2   How open learning works     10
3   What sorts of flexibility are there?     12
4   Resource-based learning     15
5   Benefits for learners and trainees     17
6   Benefits for lecturers and trainers     19
7   Benefits for employers and managers     22
8   Benefits for colleges and training providers     25
9   Which parts of the curriculum lend themselves to open learning?     28
10   Linking open learning to large-group teaching     31
11   Which learners are particularly helped?     34

**Chapter 2    Adopt, adapt or start from scratch?**     **37**
12   Adopt, adapt, or start from scratch?     39
13   Establishing the learning quality of published materials     42
14   Establishing the content relevance of published materials     45
15   What to look for in computer-based materials     48
16   Planning how to adopt     51
17   Planning how to adapt     54

**Chapter 3    Writing open learning materials**     **57**
18   Making profiles of your open learners     59
19   Tone and style for open learning     62
20   Choosing an efficient strategy     65
21   Defining intended learning outcomes     68
22   Expressing competences     71
23   Writing self-assessment questions     73
24   Writing feedback responses to structured questions     76
25   Writing multiple-choice questions     79
26   Writing feedback responses to multiple-choice questions     82
27   Writing open-ended questions and responses     84
28   Writing an introduction which works     87
29   Finishing well: reviews and summaries     89
30   Writing study guides     91

**Chapter 4   Communications and information technologies**      **94**
31   Using video for open learning                                  96
32   Using audiotapes for open learning                             99
33   Using computer-based open learning packages                   102
34   Using e-mail to support open learning                         105
35   Using computer conferencing for open learning                108
36   Using multimedia for open learning                           111
37   Using the Internet for open learning                         114

**Chapter 5   Supporting open learners**                          **117**
38   Tutoring open learners                                       119
39   Training open learning tutors                                122
40   Giving tutor feedback to open learners                       124
41   Helping open learners to develop learning skills             127
42   Helping open learners to help each other                     130
43   Mentoring open learners                                      133

**Chapter 6   Assessing open learning**                           **136**
44   Designing tutor-marked assignments                           138
45   Designing marking schemes for tutor-marked assignments       140
46   Monitoring the quality of tutor assessment                   142
47   Designing computer-marked assignments                        144
48   Designing computer-generated feedback to open learners       147
49   Designing multiple-choice exams                              149
50   Diversifying the assessment of open learners                 151
51   Piloting and adjusting open learning materials               154

**Appendix 1: A quality checklist for flexible learning materials**   **156**

**Appendix 2: Extending self-assessment: an example**            **165**

**Some further reading on open and flexible learning**            **170**

**Index**                                                         **171**

# Acknowledgements

I am particularly grateful to David Anderson (Gloscat), for very many useful suggestions and additions made to the pilot edition of this book, and also for pointing out some of the particular areas *not* addressed by this book, notably managing learning centres, designing open learning courses within college-based programmes, costing and pricing open learning, the admin and record-keeping sides of managing open learning, and tracking open learners.

I am grateful to Fiona Campbell (Napier University, Edinburgh), who noted that I have aimed my suggestions at individuals rather than institutions, and also reminded me of further things not covered by this book, including video-conferencing, and various aspects of managing the *implementation* of flexible-learning approaches in educational institutions, including planning writing schedules, corporate housestyle decisions, institutional policy making, and production of materials.

I am also grateful to Rachel Hudson (University of the West of England, Bristol), for providing me with encouraging and detailed feedback, including many ideas that I have built into this book, and also for further indications of missing dimensions from this book, notably designing open learning programmes within higher education frameworks, uses of whole-group feedback, and helping tutors and learners to make the most of face-to-face contact time. I have followed up in some detail one of her suggestions, and designed a set of suggestions on the use of audiotapes.

All of this feedback is much appreciated, but to build it all into the present book proved impossible, both in terms of the timescale for publication and the size of the book. I hope that it will be possible to persuade the colleagues mentioned above to collaborate with me on a further book on *500 Tips on Implementing Flexible Learning Delivery* building on the areas already covered in this book.

I also thank numerous participants at my workshops in the UK, Ireland, Singapore and especially New Zealand on topics spanning writing, supporting, tutoring and assessing open and flexible learning, for developing my thinking on all of the issues addressed in this book. I am also grateful to even more students, with whom I have worked on developing their study skills approaches to open and flexible learning, for constantly reminding me of the need to keep effective and successful learning at the forefront of our planning.

# Introduction

## What is this book about?

Although the title uses the umbrella term 'open and flexible learning' the book could equally well be said to be about resource-based learning, or simply student-centred approaches to learning. In this book, my aim is to provide practical, useful suggestions for staff in educational and training organizations who are moving towards increasing use of open or flexible learning. Whether you are already involved, or just thinking about starting to use open learning, I hope that you will find suggestions in this book which will not only save you time and energy, but will enhance the quality of the learning experience which your learners draw from flexible learning.

Successive chapters address:

1   **Terminology, contexts and benefits:** where I have tried to introduce and demystify some of the many terms used in the field of open learning. I have also spelled out some of the benefits which can be claimed for well-designed open learning provision, not just to learners themselves, but also to lecturers, employers and organizations.

2   **Adopt, adapt, or start from scratch:** essentially about a range of decisions that need to be made regarding making use of existing resource materials, or deciding whether you do really need to start from scratch and create entirely new open learning materials.

3   **Writing open learning materials:** where I offer a range of suggestions for those who do indeed decide to create new open learning materials. Many of these suggestions also apply to those who may be adapting existing materials, or writing study guidance material to support students working flexibly on resource-based learning elements of their studies.

4   **Communications and information technologies:** where I offer some suggestions about how to ensure that effective learning is promoted using a range of communications and information technology formats and processes. The importance of these technologies has increased rapidly in recent years and seems set to continue to do so exponentially. It is vitally important that creators of new learning materials do not get carried away with the technology, however, and remain tuned in to the optimum ways that computers and electronic communication can indeed enhance learning and enrich feedback, both to and from learners themselves.

5   **Supporting open learners:** a chapter which is about people. The majority of provision of open and flexible learning is supported by tutors or mentors or both. Learners themselves are people, and need to develop human skills to make the most of the learning resources they work with.

6   **Assessing open learning:** which for many open learners is related to their most important target. Most open or flexible learning is not undertaken for its own sake, but as a way to gain qualifications or accreditation of some kind. Sometimes, assessment can be well tuned to enhancing and enriching learning, but care needs to be taken that assessment is valid, fair, reliable and does not demotivate learners.

# What is this book *not* about?

The suggestions in this book don't go into detail about the following aspects of open and flexible learning:

*   setting up and managing learning resource centres (although I have provided detailed suggestions which should help in *choosing* the materials that are housed in such centres, and some advice about supporting the learners who use them);

*   strategic planning of institutional approaches to employ flexible learning to deliver an increased proportion of the curriculum to growing student numbers, or to make better use of resources in circumstances where budgets are tight (although many of my suggestions will provide a *basis* for informed decisions in institutional policy making forums);

*   costing and pricing of open learning provision, including costs associated with the in-house production and reproduction of open learning materials. (I feel that the true costs of implementing flexible learning development are frequently underestimated, and that where flexible learning is introduced for supposed financial reasons rather than to deliver better learning experiences to students, such development rarely succeeds!)

It may well be sensible to plan a further volume in the same format to address these issues, but I feel that for each of the areas above to be addressed successfully depends on the development of a shared attitude to, and understanding of, the principles of best practice in flexible learning. I have, therefore, tried in this book to address these principles in detail, to pave the way towards effective institutional development of flexible learning.

# How can this book be used?

In writing this book, I have kept in mind several possibilities and I hope that the book will serve different people in different ways, including:

- practical pointers on open and flexible learning, if you are simply too busy to spend time reading the detailed or theoretical accounts that are available in the relevant literature, and need a source of 'how to do it' suggestions which you can try out at short notice;

- a dip-in resource if you are already involved in creating, supporting or delivering open or flexible learning, which will provide you with some suggestions you can try out straightaway, and others which you can reflect upon and perhaps adapt to your own circumstances or plan into your future work;

- a set of starting points for discussion by teams of people who are planning to implement open or flexible learning, where I trust that individual sets of suggestions will provide an agenda on which to base your decisions and action plans;

- a practical, pragmatic, awareness-raising source if you are new to open and flexible learning and are thinking of working out for yourself whether you will become involved in using such approaches;

- an aid to institutional thinking about policies linked to developing student-centred learning provision, and about the role that flexible learning can play in the wider scene of institutional delivery;

- if you are a lecturer or trainer working primarily in face-to-face contexts with learners, I hope that my suggestions in this book will provide you with useful food for thought and help you to interrogate aspects of your own practice.

I conclude the book with two appendices.

**'A quality checklist for flexible learning materials'** summarizes many of the main points that I have made in the book, collecting them into 40 questions with which to interrogate the quality of open and flexible learning resource materials, whether print-based or electronic. This checklist should be useful when making decisions about adopting, or adapting, existing open learning materials. It is also intended to provide a self-assessment tool with which creators of new open and flexible materials can interrogate (in the comfort of privacy) their practice.

**'Extending self-assessment'** where I offer a short specimen questionnaire, designed for open learners to complete and submit along with tutor-marked assignments, causing them to reflect further on their work. The main purpose, however, is to use this self-assessment as the basis of dialogue with their tutors, so that the feedback that learners receive from them has even greater value and relevance. My questionnaire is not intended to be used as it stands, but to be adapted by tutors to reflect the nature and content of individual assignments, so that both the quality and the relevance to students of the resulting dialogue can be enhanced.

# Chapter 1 Terminology, contexts, benefits

1    What sorts of learning?
2    How open learning works
3    What sorts of flexibility are there?
4    Resource-based learning
5    Benefits for learners and trainees
6    Benefits for lecturers and trainers
7    Benefits for employers and managers
8    Benefits for colleges and training providers
9    Which parts of the curriculum lend themselves to open learning?
10   Linking open learning to large-group teaching
11   Which learners are particularly helped?

This chapter is about putting open and flexible learning into context. I start by looking at some of the overlapping terms which are in common use for learning situations. These terms, besides the most common ones 'open' and 'flexible', include distance, individualized, and independent learning, as well as supported self-study. The term 'resource-based learning' is coming into its own now, and just about all varieties of open and flexible learning could be said to be resource-based (as indeed, are many traditional college-based programmes, where the resources include textbooks, journals and handout materials). The acronym RBL is in common use for resource-based learning, and also represents *Responsibility*-Based Learning, which applies strongly to any kind of open and flexible learning as well. This book could well have been called *500 Tips on Resource-Based Learning*.

The next section is about how open learning (or most of the other kinds already mentioned) actually work, and this is followed by a short exploration of the various degrees of flexibility which can be introduced into open or flexible learning provision.

After a short exploration of the range covered by the term 'Resource-based learning', the next four sections look at some of the benefits which accrue from flexibility. Open learning brings different potential benefits to different target audiences, so I have treated separately the benefits for learners, lecturers, employers and institutions.

The next section addresses the question 'Which parts of the curriculum lend themselves to open learning?' In practice, just about *any* element of the curriculum can be delivered through open learning, but it is important to have good reasons for choosing those elements that are *best* delivered flexibly.

The next section is about linking open learning to large-group teaching. In many parts of further and higher education, open and flexible approaches are being used to replace some face-to-face time with students because of growing student numbers, diminishing budgets and overworked staff. It is important to make sure that the open learning elements are not seen as something different from, or less important than, the class-based parts of a course. Linking open learning to lectures is the best way to show students that it counts.

I end this chapter by looking at the particular categories of learners who can derive benefits from open and flexible learning. The list embraces most learners, when open learning is used to address their respective needs and attitudes.

# 1

# What sorts of learning?

Open learning, like most aspects of education and training, has its own set of terms and phrases with particular meanings in given contexts. The following descriptions of ten kinds of learning should help you clarify the meanings of some of the terminology used about the sorts of learning that are addressed in this book. It should be noted that the umbrella term 'open learning' tends to be the one which embraces or includes all the rest, although 'flexible learning' may well be the most appropriate general term.

It is important not to be limited by any of the definitions or terminologies shown below, and to remember that they all address, in slightly different contexts, a common set of principles, including:

- putting the learner in the driving seat;
- giving students ownership of their learning;
- tailoring study programmes to meet learners' individual requirements;
- a philosophy of teaching and learning, not a technology;
- changed roles of learners and tutors towards active participation of *both* in the processes of learning.

1   **Open learning.** This is normally taken to mean provision for learners where they have some control regarding how they learn, where they learn, when they learn and the pace at which they learn. Open learning sometimes also involves learners having some control of what they learn and how (or if) their learning will be assessed.

2   **Distance learning.** This is the term usually applied to open learning which takes place at a distance from the provider of the learning materials. Examples include the Open University in the UK, and correspondence courses throughout the world.

3   **Flexible learning.** This term includes the sorts of learning involved in open and distance learning provision, but additionally relates to learning pathways in traditional schools, colleges and universities, where learners have some control of the time, place, pace and processes of their study of particular parts of their curriculum. It is sometimes regarded as a management tool for institutions, with its uses including removing barriers to access, improving choice for students and widening participation in further and higher education. Flexible learning has become another umbrella term, usually in the context of structured college-based systems of resource-based learning and learning support.

4   **Individualized learning.** This refers to any kind of learning where it is envisaged that learners work largely on their own, including many open, flexible or distance learning programmes.

5   **Resource-based learning.** This normally refers to learning pathways where learners are supported mainly by learning resource materials, which can range from textbooks to open learning packages, and can range from print-based to computer-based formats. It includes just about all learning situations that go under the names of open or flexible learning.

6   **Supported self-study.** This term is usually used to describe open, distance or flexible learning programmes, where learners work with the aid of learning resource materials of one kind or another, and are supported in their learning by printed or computer-based briefing and guidance materials and/or by tutorial provision. In sixth-form school contexts, the role of the tutor in the process is given much more prominence.

7   **Independent learning.** This term is usually employed to emphasize the freedom of learners studying by open, distance or flexible learning processes, using either print-based or computer-based learning resources, and supported by printed briefings or human tutors. Interpretations of independent learning include the use of learning contracts or negotiated learning agreements, with negotiated self-assessment of students' achievement of their agreed outcomes.

8   **Student-centred learning.** Ideally all learning should be student-centred! However, this term is often used to describe any or all of the learning formats mentioned above, where the learning processes and learning resource materials can be claimed to have been designed to be as relevant and supportive as possible to the learners using them.

9    **Computer-assisted learning.** This is one of a range of related terms, also including computer-based training. All such learning or training can be considered to have features common to other open and flexible learning formats, but in addition include the use of computers or multimedia hardware.

10   **Interactive learning.** A key feature of well-designed open or flexible learning materials is that learners interact with them. In short, learners are given things to do as a primary means to help them learn, and are then provided with feedback to help them see how they have done (or what they may have done incorrectly). Many sections in this book address how best to get learning-by-doing in progress and ways of ensuring that feedback is appropriate and effective.

# 2

# How open learning works

In this section I offer ten suggestions regarding the key features of effective open learning provision. Matters arising from these suggestions are further developed extensively throughout this book, so the factors described below should only be taken as a starting point.

1   **Open learning should be learning-by-doing.** Almost all learning happens best when coupled with experience, practice, trial-and-error and hands-on activity. Even the learning of theories and concepts needs practice in applying them and trying them out.

2   **Open learning depends on feedback to learners.** All learners need to find out how their learning is going. The levels of appropriateness and quality of the feedback that open learners receive as they learn-by-doing are the hallmarks of the most effective open learning materials, whether print-based or computer-based.

3   **Open learning needs to address learners' 'want' to learn.** Effective open learning materials work by enhancing learners' motivation, such as by being user-friendly, easy to follow and supportive – even when the subject matter is difficult and complex.

4   **Open learning needs to satisfy well-articulated needs.** Learners need to be able to see what an open learning pathway can achieve for them, and this should relate to ambitions or intentions that learners relate to strongly.

5   **Open learning needs to give learners every opportunity to make sense of what they are learning.** Rote learning is of limited value, and it is important to help learners to 'get their heads around' new concepts and ideas. The quality of the feedback provided by open learning materials, and by tutors or trainers supporting open learning, is crucial in helping open learners to develop an appropriate level of understanding of what they are learning.

6    **Open learning should be designed to help people to learn at their own pace.** Many of the problems with traditional forms of teaching, training and instruction arise because of the pace being too fast or too slow for learners. Open learning materials and formats can give learners a great deal of freedom in the pace they take, even when deadlines or cut-off dates need to be set for associated assessment.

7    **Open learning is often designed to allow people to learn at their own choices of place.** Print-based packages are usually designed to be complete in themselves, or to work alongside existing reference materials, which can be used at home, or at work or in any other suitable learning environment. Computer-based packages offer more limited choices of place, although increasingly learners are likely to have suitable equipment at home as well as at their workplace or study location.

8    **Open learning is sometimes designed without specific needs for prerequisite knowledge or experience.** For example, in the UK, Open University Foundation Courses are essentially open to anyone. When learners do need starting competences or knowledge, it is important that such prerequisites are spelled out clearly at the start of the packages or in the promotional literature relating to them.

9    **Most open learning packages are backed up by some form of tutor support.** This is particularly important when the achievements of learners need to be assessed and accredited in some way. Sometimes open learning programmes are continuously assessed by tutors, or may lead towards formal exams, or use a combination of tutor assessment and exams.

10   **Increasingly, open learning packages use a variety of learning media.** Combinations of printed interactive materials, textual reference materials, computer-based interactive packages, video recordings, CD-ROM interactive packages and electronic communication media add to the richness and variety of the learning experiences of open learners.

# 3

# What sorts of flexibility are there?

Whether we think about open learning as used in distance-learning programmes or flexible learning as may be used for particular elements within traditional college-based programmes, there are several different aspects to flexibility. The three most common reasons learners themselves give for selecting open and flexible learning pathways are:

- to fit in with work commitments;
- to accommodate family commitments;
- to enable them to work at their own pace, place and times of their choosing.

Not all open or flexible learning programmes can address all of the factors outlined above. However, the following descriptions may alert you to which aspects of flexibility you particularly want to address in your own provision.

1    **Flexibility can mean freedom of start dates.** Many open learning programmes are described as 'roll-on, roll-off' systems. The key feature here is that learners can more or less start at any time of the year and finish when they are ready. There may be difficulties incorporating such an approach when open or flexible learning is being used for elements within college-based programmes, not least as most educational or training institutions do not operate on a 52-week year. However, even on semesterized, modular frameworks there remains some leeway for flexibility regarding start and stop times for at least some modules.

2    **Flexibility can mean freedom of entry levels.** It is important to spell out clearly any pre-requisite knowledge or skills, so that all open learners can assess whether they are able to progress on to working with each package. However, open learning can be designed so that some learners will need

to work through the whole of a package while others, who are already more advanced (or more familiar with the topic), can skip the introductory materials in the package and start their work at the point where they are learning new things from it.

3   **Flexibility can give learners some choice of how much support they use.** Tutor support may well be available to all of the learners on a programme, but some may make little use of this and still succeed without difficulty. Some open learners prefer to work on their own and rise well to the challenge of sorting out their own problems. Those learners who most need tutor support can then be accommodated.

4   **Flexibility can give some freedom regarding students' level of motivation.** Open learners can decide whether to put in the minimum amount of work to be 'safe', or whether to follow up strong interests and go much deeper into what they are learning.

5   **Flexibility can mean freedom of pace.** This is one of the most attractive hallmarks of many open learning programmes. Especially when studied by mature, part-time students freedom of pace may be an essential feature, allowing them to fit their learning into busy or unpredictable work patterns.

6   **Flexibility can allow freedom of location.** Open learning can allow students to continue their studies while away from the institution on work placements, or on vacation or even when confined to home by temporary illness.

7   **Flexibility can mean freedom of choice of learning environment.** Students can have more choice about whether they work in a library or learning resource centre, or at home or wherever they feel comfortable. They can make their own choices about whether they prefer to work in scholastic silence, or with background sounds of their preference.

8   **Flexibility can allow learners freedom to determine how important a part information technology will play in their studies.** While for some open learning it may be deemed necessary to involve students in using communications and information technology, for some students this can be a significant hurdle. With flexible learning, it can usually be arranged that there is more than one way of achieving most of the outcomes successfully.

9    **Flexibility can mean freedom of end points.** In some open learning systems, students can go in for assessments (tutor-marked, computer-marked and even formal exams) more or less when they feel that they are ready for assessment. This can allow high fliers to try the assessments without spending much time studying the materials concerned, or learners who find the material more demanding to wait until they are confident that they can succeed with the assessed components.

10   **Flexibility can allow learners to work collaboratively or on their own.** Some learners may not have much opportunity to work collaboratively, for example, isolated students on distance learning programmes. For them, it may, however, be possible to use electronic communication to allow them to make efficient (and cheap) contact with each other. For college-based students working through flexible learning elements alongside class-based ones, it is worthwhile to encourage them to collaborate, as they can often give each other useful feedback and help each other to make sense of the more difficult ideas and concepts.

# 4

# Resource-based learning

Resource-based learning (RBL) is a term in sufficiently common use that an acronym exists from it. Perhaps the acronym should also represent 'Responsibility-Based Learning', as in all varieties of resource-based learning, more responsibility rests with learners themselves than in traditional teaching–learning situations. In the strictest sense, all learning could be considered to be resource-based, where the resources include handouts, lecture notes, textbooks, journal articles and human tutors. However, the term resource-based learning is usually used in circumstances where the learning that takes place from these, or other types of learning resources, is somewhat different from that which happens in traditional teaching–learning formats. Resource-based learning could be regarded as another umbrella term and spans just about all that goes under the names of open or flexible learning. Many of the learning processes involved in all forms of open learning are resource-based. The following suggestions may help you to put resource-based learning into context.

1   **Resource-based learning can be considered to be open or flexible in nature.** Open learning packages are learning resources in their own right, whether they are print-based, computer-based or multimedia in design. The learning that happens in resource-based learning usually opens up some freedom of time and pace, if not always that of place.

2   **Resource-based learning suggests that the subject content is provided to learners through materials rather than via teaching.** The term 'resource-based' is often used as an 'opposite' to 'taught'. Having said that, good practice in face-to-face teaching and learning often depends on learners working with learning resources during sessions, as well as outside formal contact time.

3   **The learning that happens in learning resource centres is usually considered to be resource-based.** This suggests that resource-based learning is often based on the sorts of open learning resources which are best located in a particular centre, with the opportunity of technical or tutor support as may be necessary, rather than materials that learners

take with them to their homes or workplaces. In practice, resource-based learning is regarded as being delivered *through* such centres and includes considerations of the physical environments experienced by learners.

4    **Learning resources can be quite traditional in nature, too.** With suitable study guides or briefing notes, resources such as textbooks, videos, audiotapes and journals can all be part of resource-based learning programmes, either when located in learning resources centres or libraries, or when issued to or borrowed by learners.

5    **Students may require appropriate induction into how resource-based learning elements in their courses should best be approached.** In particular, it is important for learners to be aware of the ways that the resources are designed to help them to learn, and how to keep track of their own progress.

6    **Resource-based learning usually accommodates a considerable amount of learning-by-doing.** Resources should provide learners with opportunities to practise and to learn by making mistakes in the relative comfort of privacy.

7    **Resource-based learning depends on learners being provided with feedback on how their learning is going.** This feedback can be provided by human tutors, or by interactive elements within the learning resources, where feedback to learners may be provided in print or on-screen.

8    **Clearly expressed learning outcomes are important in all kinds of resource-based learning.** There may not be tutor support available at all times, and that tone-of-voice, emphasis of tone and facial expression may not be available to help learners work out exactly what it is that they are expected to be able to do as they work with the resource materials. This means that the wording of the intended learning outcomes is crucial.

9    **Assessment criteria need to be clearly stated along with resource-based learning.** Learners take important cues from the expected performance criteria, and indicators of the kinds (and extent) of the evidence they should accumulate to demonstrate that they have learnt successfully from resource-based learning materials.

10   **Resource-based learning often needs appropriate face-to-face debriefing.** It can be very worthwhile to reserve a whole-class session to review an element of resource-based learning and to answer learners' questions about the topics covered in this way. Such group sessions can also be used to gain useful feedback about the strengths and weaknesses of the materials themselves.

# 5

# Benefits for learners and trainees

'What's in it for me?' is a natural question for open learners to ask, especially if their previous education or training has been delivered using conventional or traditional teaching and learning processes. It is important that learners are alerted to the benefits that can accompany open learning pathways. The following are some of the principal benefits open learning can offer them, written along the lines that you could explain them to learners.

1   **You can learn when you want to.** This means that you can make use of down-time at work, or at any time of the day or night when you can find time to study. You do not have to wait for timetabled lectures or training sessions. You may even be able to start and finish your studies at dates of your own choosing, rather than have to fit in with course start dates and finish dates.

2   **You can learn where you want to.** With print-based (and some computer-based) packages, you can choose your own preferred learning environment. Better still, you can always have some of your learning materials with you, allowing you to do at least some studying in each of many different locations – at home, at work, in colleges, in libraries, on trains, in waiting rooms – almost anywhere.

3   **You can learn at your own pace.** You do not have to worry about how fast you are learning, or whether other people seem to be faster than you. When you find something difficult, you can simply spend more time on it.

4   **You know where you're heading.** Good open learning materials have well expressed learning outcomes. You can go back and look again at these at any time to remind you of what you are trying to achieve. You can read them as many times as you need to, so that you get a real feeling for what is involved in them.

5    **You can see what the standards are.** Self-assessment questions and assignments will give you a good idea of the level you should aim to meet. You can scan these in advance to alert you to what is coming up.

6    **You can get things wrong in the comfort of privacy.** Learning by making mistakes is a productive way to learn most things. With self-assessment questions and exercises, you can afford to find out which things you are confused about. When you know exactly what the problems are, you are usually well on your way to solving them.

7    **You get feedback on how your learning is going.** The feedback responses to self-assessment questions will confirm whether you are getting the hang of the material. When you get something wrong, the feedback may well help you to find out *why* you did so, and will not just tell you what the correct answer should have been.

8    **You can decide what to skip altogether.** For example, if you think you can already achieve a particular learning outcome, you can have a go straightaway at the related self-assessment questions or exercises. If you know you can already do these successfully, you can skip them and go straight to the feedback responses to check that you would have succeeded.

9    **You can keep practising till you master difficult things.** When you have problems with self-assessment questions and exercises, you can have another go at them a little later on to check whether you still know how to deal with them.

10   **You can stop when you are tired or bored.** Successful learning tends to happen in bytes rather than megabytes. When you're flagging, you can have a break, or go backwards or forwards to some other part of your learning materials that you find more interesting.

11   **You become more confident.** Open learning helps you to develop your own self-esteem and autonomy as a learner, and this helps you to make the most of each and every learning opportunity you meet.

# 6

# Benefits for lecturers and trainers

If you are normally involved in delivering face-to-face education or training, to move towards incorporating flexible or open learning elements you need to be able to see significant benefits for yourself as well as for your learners. It is important to be able to convince yourself, as well as any traditionally-minded colleagues, about the potential of open learning. This includes having replies for colleagues who may think that 'my students will never learn this way', or 'I love to teach, and my students always do so well, why throw that away?' If you need to enthuse fellow lecturers or trainers about the benefits of open learning, you need to be able to offer them something that they will appreciate. Here are some suggestions as a starting point.

1   **You won't have to teach the same things over and over again.** With open or flexible learning materials, the things that you teach most often (and perhaps sometimes get bored with teaching) are likely to be the first areas which you decide to package up into open learning materials or flexible learning options.

2   **You won't have to explain the same things over and over again.** In face-to-face work with learners, it often happens that you seem to be explaining repeatedly the same things to different people. The same mistakes and misconceptions occur frequently, and you may lose enthusiasm for putting learners right about these. With open or flexible learning, such areas represent ideal development ground for self-assessment questions and feedback responses, where you are able to package up your experience of explaining such things to learners into a form where they can benefit from your explanations without you having to keep delivering them.

3   **Flexible learning can help you to deliver more curriculum.** With open learning much of the actual learning will be done by learners in their own time, and your task becomes to help them to navigate the course of learning resource materials rather than to go through all of the curriculum directly with them. This can be particularly useful if you already feel under pressure about getting through all of your curriculum with students.

4   **Flexible learning can help your learners to develop important skills beyond the curriculum.** Such skills include working with learning resources independently, practising self-assessment and evaluation, becoming better at time management and task management, prioritising the relative importance of different parts of the syllabus and using fellow learners as a resource. All of these skills are useful in the world of work and are valued by employers. Flexible learning provides your learners not only with a chance to practise and develop these skills, but opportunities to accumulate evidence of their development as autonomous learners.

5   **Open learning can refresh your practice.** Getting involved in open learning causes staff to re-examine their approaches to teaching, learning and assessment. For example, fresh attention is often paid to identifying learning outcomes, and to expressing these in clear unambiguous language that open learners can understand. This can lead to parallel refinements in face-to-face work with students or trainees. The key principles of good practice in open learning extend readily to face-to-face education.

6   **You can focus your skills and experience on areas where learners really *need* your help.** Since flexible learning materials can cover most of the anticipated questions and problems that learners normally have, your role of supporting open learners moves towards being an expert witness for those questions where they really need your experience to help them.

7   **You can move towards being a learning manager.** This helps you to have more time and energy to focus on individual students' needs and difficulties, rather than simply delivering the content of the curriculum. Some of the most satisfying parts of the work of lecturers and trainers are seeing that individuals have been helped and developed.

8   **You may be able to escape from some things you don't enjoy teaching.** You can do this by packaging up into open learning formats those parts of your syllabus. This has benefits for your learners as well as for you, as if you are teaching something you are fed up with, the chances of them becoming enthused by such topics diminishes, and their learning is unlikely to be very successful.

9   **Open learning can make your job more secure.** Although many educators and trainers fear that they could make themselves redundant by moving towards open learning, in practice the reverse tends to happen. Staff who can generate or support open learning often find themselves even more valued. The diversification of their skills opens up new ways in which they can deliver learning and training.

10  **It is less of a disaster if you're ill!** In face-to-face programmes, it can be a nightmare if you are unable to deliver important parts of the curriculum, or even if you lose your voice and cannot give lectures. When open learning materials are available, it is often possible to use these at times when you are unable to, for example, give a lecture or run a training session. It is much easier to brief a colleague to give your class some briefings about using their learning resource materials, than to hand over a lecture or presentation to someone else.

11  **You can spend more of your time getting the assessment side of things right.** From your learners' point of view, assessment may well be the most important dimension. Busy lecturers often do not have as much time as they would wish either to design good, valid assessments or to mark them. When flexible learning is used to reduce face-to-face delivery time, some of this time can usefully be diverted into paying more detailed attention to assessment.

# 7

# Benefits for employers and managers

The benefits of open learning are well appreciated by those employers or managers who have been successful open learners themselves – a rapidly increasing group. They need no explanations about why flexible learning may be offered instead of, or as part of, a college-based programme. For some employers and managers, however, open and flexible learning seems rather different to the way that they remember their own education or training. Some of them still equate effective learning with attending classes. Since they may need convincing about the benefits of flexible learning before sponsoring their staff to participate in such programmes, the following benefits may be useful to you if your role includes justifying open learning provision to such people.

1   **Your staff will have a better chance of learning relevant things.** The flexibility provided by open learning means that it is often possible to choose training materials that are directly suited to learning needs relating to the workplace.

2   **You can see the relevance of each learning programme.** Because open and flexible learning programmes are normally based on clearly stated intended learning outcomes, you can check how useful the achievement of these outcomes by your staff will be for your own organization.

3   **Open learning is based on learning-by-doing.** Therefore, your staff will be learning more from practising and applying the skills concepts and ideas that they are encountering than might have been the case if they had merely attended courses where tutors talked about the subjects being learnt.

4    **Open learning materials provide feedback to each learner.** In college-based programmes, learners may have to wait for feedback on their progress; with open learning they get much of the feedback at once from the learning resource materials, while their attempts at tasks, questions and exercises are still fresh in their minds.

5    **Most open learning programmes use tutor support.** At best, this support is focused towards those aspects of their studies where learners need human judgement from an expert witness, and away from routine feedback on common problems, which can be built into the learning resource materials. In effect, this can mean that the human interventions of tutor support are much more significant and useful than they sometimes are on a taught course.

6    **You can judge the standard of the training.** Open learning materials include self-assessment tasks and exercises, and tutor-marked assignments, all of which help you to see the standard to which your staff are being trained. The assessed components of open learning materials and programmes help you to monitor the actual level to which the intended learning outcomes can be expected to be achieved by your staff.

7    **Employees will develop themselves as autonomous learners.** This is one of the most significant payoffs of open learning. The skills which open learners necessarily develop or improve upon include time management, task management, taking charge of their own learning, learning from print-based or computer-based resource materials, as well as taking most of the responsibility for preparing themselves for assessment. All of these skills make people more employable and more resourceful.

8    **There is less time off the job.** Open and flexible learning allows staff to learn in the workplace, during down-time or quiet periods, as well as to extend their studies to home-based learning. The amount of travelling time to a training centre or college is reduced or even eliminated.

9    **Open learning helps your organization to cope with the unexpected.** When urgent needs demand that staff cannot be released to attend timetabled training programmes, open learning allows them to catch up on their studies when the immediate requirement for their presence has been accommodated. This allows you to reduce the occurrence of key staff being unavailable for unanticipated important work, due to being off-site on training programmes.

10   **You can make further use of learning resource materials.** When some of
     your staff have successfully completed open learning courses or elements,
     the materials that they have learnt from may still be available to you to
     spread to other staff. The resource materials are much more permanent
     than the transient experiences of staff attending lectures or training
     workshops. It is much more difficult to cascade live training than open
     learning. That means, however, that the valuable tutor-support elements
     of open learning may not be able to be extended to other staff working
     through the learning materials on their own.

# 8

# Benefits for colleges and training providers

Many colleges in further and higher education are moving towards making open and flexible learning a more important part of their operations. Similar developments have affected training centres in many organizations and industries. This trend, however, is not always being done for the best of reasons. In particular, the view that flexible learning can reduce staff costs is fraught with danger. The following list of benefits of open learning may be useful to you if you need to inform senior managers or policy makers in colleges or training centres about *good* reasons for introducing flexibility in delivery.

1   **Open learning widens the range of training needs that can be addressed.** At times when the viability of courses and programmes depends more sharply on economics, many useful programmes become untenable for financial reasons. Flexible learning can prove more cost effective in such cases, while maintaining a desirable breadth of provision.

2   **Open learning can make your organization more competitive.** This is more to do with the breadth of learning needs or training needs that can be addressed, than about the unit cost averaged out over students or trainees. Competitiveness is also linked to your organization's ability to respond to diverse requirements regarding the time scales of provision, and the extent of support required by learners.

3   **Open learning meets accepted national agendas and targets.** In the UK and elsewhere, government policies are exhorting providers to address widening participation in learning, and exploiting communications and information technologies, as well as to address the professionalism of those involved in teaching and learning management. Open and flexible learning development can be directly relevant to achieving such targets.

4   **Strategic commitment by senior managers to open learning can underpin success.** When open learning is supported from the top down in an institution, the other requirements tend to fall into place, including appropriate information technology formats for flexible learning delivery, relevant staff training provision, and well thought out resources deployment.

5   **Open learning causes fruitful staff development.** One of the most significant payoffs of becoming involved in delivering or supporting open learning is that staff look again at how best to support *learning*, rather than just how to teach or to train. Many staff report that things they found out through supporting open learners change their practice significantly with face-to-face students or trainees.

6   **Open learning helps develop a multi-skilled staff.** Tutors and trainers who get involved in designing or supporting open learning learn a variety of new skills, which can pay dividends to the operation of colleges and training providers. For some staff, the new challenges and demands associated with designing and delivering open and flexible learning enrich their professional practice and bring new enthusiasm to their work.

7   **Open learning increases the variety of roles needed by college staff or trainers.** This can mean, for example, that someone who has problems delivering face-to-face sessions may be found a valuable role in some other aspect of supporting learning, or designing new materials, or spending time assessing open learners' work and giving them feedback in writing or by electronic communication.

8   **Open learning is not about dispensing with people.** When used wisely, open learning can be a means of giving staff more opportunity to do the things that are *best* done by people. Much of the routine transmission of information to students or trainees can be achieved using learning resource materials. This gives your staff more time to concentrate on applying high level human skills to support students and to exercise their professional judgement.

9   **Open learning can make more cost-effective use of your resources.** For example, open learning can continue for almost all weeks of the year, making good use of learning resources centres, libraries, computing facilities as well as of staff. Care needs to be taken, however, to ensure that all staff have adequate opportunities both to plan and take holidays and other kinds of absence, such as attending training programmes themselves, or participating in conferences and meetings.

10   **Open learning can reduce peak demand levels.** For example, with 'roll-on, roll-off' open learning programmes (or flexible learning elements in conventional programmes), learners are not restricted to starting at a particular time of the year or being assessed at another fixed time. There can be choices of start and finish dates and fast-track possibilities for the most able learners, as well as 'crawler-lane provision' for learners whose time may be very limited.

11   **Open learning allows more opportunity to review assessment standards, instruments and processes.** Because the curriculum delivered by open learning is public, with clearly framed statements of intended learning outcomes, it is necessary to ensure that the assessment associated with open learning is not only reliable but also valid and robust. Some of the time saved from face-to-face delivery of information can usefully be diverted into refining and testing assessment formats.

12   **Open learning helps move towards being a learning organization.** The student-centredness of open learning can become a driving force extending throughout the organization and transforming traditional face-to-face delivery, as well as support offered to learners. It can cause attitude changes which break down the barriers between managers, teaching and support staff.

# 9

# Which parts of the curriculum lend themselves to open learning?

Whether you are designing an open learning package for use at a distance or for use within a college-based programme, it is worthwhile to think about which parts of the curriculum best lend themselves to an open or flexible approach. It is useful to start your open learning writing with such parts and, perhaps better still, to experiment first with adapting existing resources covering such curriculum areas towards a flexible learning format. The following suggestions show that such starting points can be based on several different considerations, and are often linked to ways that open learning can augment face-to-face college-based programmes.

1   **Important background material.** In face-to-face programmes, a considerable amount of time is often spent near the start, getting everyone up to speed with essential knowledge or skills, to the annoyance of the learners who already have these. Making such information the basis of an open learning package can allow those people who need to cover this material before the whole group starts to do so in their own time and at their own pace, without holding up the rest of the group.

2   **'Need to know before...' material.** For example, when different learners will be attempting different practical exercises at the same time, it could take far too long to cover all the prerequisite material with the whole group before introducing practical work. Designing separate, short open learning elements to pave the way to each practical exercise can allow these to be issued to learners so that the practical work can be started much earlier.

3 **'Remedial material'.** In many courses, there are problem topics which can hold up a whole class while the difficulties are addressed by lecturers or tutors. This can lead to time being wasted, particularly by those learners for whom there are no problems with the parts concerned. The availability of open learning packages addressing such areas can allow these packages to be used only by those learners who need them, in their own time, so that the progress of the whole group is not impeded.

4 **'Nice-to-know' material.** While 'need-to-know' material is more important, open learning elements can be particularly useful to address 'nice-to-know' material, and giving such material to learners without spending too much face-to-face time on it. This allows contact time to be saved for helping learners with the really important material and for addressing their problems.

5 **Much repeated material.** If you find yourself often covering the same ground, perhaps with different groups of learners in different contexts or courses, it can be worth thinking about packaging up such material in open learning formats. If you yourself get bored with things you often teach, you are not going to pass on much enthusiasm for these topics to your learners, and it can be mutually beneficial to invest your energy into creating an alternative flexible learning pathway to cover such material.

6 **Material which is best 'learnt by doing'.** Open learning is based on learners answering questions, doing tasks and exercises. Therefore, a useful starting point for an open learning package is to base it on the sorts of activities that you may already be giving your face-to-face students. Standard assignments and activities already in use in traditionally delivered courses and programmes may be adapted quite easily for open learning usage, and have the strong benefit that they are already tried and tested elements of the curriculum.

7 **Material where learners need individual feedback on their progress.** A vital element of open learning is the feedback that learners receive when they have attempted to answer questions, or had a try at exercises and activities. The sorts of feedback that you may already give your face-to-face learners can be packaged up into open learning materials.

8 **Material that you don't like to teach!** It can be tempting to turn such elements of the curriculum into open learning materials, where learners can work on them individually (or in untutored groups), and using face-to-face time more efficiently to address any problems that learners find, rather than to teach them from scratch.

9 **Material that learners find hard to grasp first time.** In most subjects there are such areas. Developing open learning materials addressing these means that learners can go through them on their own, as many times as they need. Effectively, the open learning material becomes their teacher or trainer. Learners can then work through such materials at their own pace and can practise with the learning materials until they master them.

10 **Material which may be needed later, at short notice.** It is often the case that some topics are only really needed by learners quite some time after they may have been covered in a course or programme. When such materials are turned into open learning formats, learners can polish up their grip on the topics involved just when they need to.

# 10

# Linking open learning to large-group teaching

Implementing flexible learning with small groups of students poses few particular problems, provided the learning materials are of good quality and there is appropriate support for students. However, student numbers continue to grow in college-based courses in many disciplines, and resource constraints have meant that face-to-face time with students has to be more limited than formerly. Open and flexible learning materials and pathways can take some of the pressure away, but need to be firmly linked with mainstream teaching, otherwise students may feel that the open learning elements are peripheral. The following suggestions aim to help you to ensure that such pathways and materials are worth the time and effort that is involved in creating them.

1 **Decide which parts of the syllabus to switch to open learning mode.** A previous section of this book gave suggestions about which parts of the curriculum in general lend themselves to open learning delivery. A later section looks at the categories of learners likely to benefit from flexible learning. Combine these two agendas to work out in the context of your own lecture programme which will be the best parts to use, maximising the benefits to the most appropriate cross-section of your class.

2 **Work out the best things to do in lecture times.** It is becoming increasingly common to design open learning materials to replace some of the material that was formerly handled in lectures. It is important to put the remaining occasions when a whole group is together to optimum usage. Such usage includes guiding and supporting learners who are doing some or most of their learning from open learning materials.

3 **Make sure that your learners do not regard the open learning as an optional extra.** For example, use lecture time to explain to the whole group which learning outcomes are being covered by the flexible learning materials, and what the balance is between what will be covered in class and the learning that students are required to do on their own.

4    **Reserve some class time to answer students' questions about the open learning material.** It can be useful to use large-group time to collect and address problems that students find, and a more efficient use of time than trying to deal with students' questions by appointment or in surgery times.

5    **Use lectures to 'spotlight' rather than to 'cover'.** Decide on the really important elements of the course, where it is worth the whole group having a shared learning experience along with the opportunity for questions and discussion. Explain to learners which parts you are going to spotlight in this way and why. This helps them to see that they have the responsibility for learning the parts that are not going to be spotlighted in this way.

6    **Consider using elements of the open learning material as prerequisite for particular lecture sessions.** For example, you can 'require' students to have worked through a particular section of their materials before attending a specific lecture, and structuring the session such that learners who have not done this feel sufficiently disadvantaged or embarrassed that they do not put themselves in such a position in future.

7    **Consider building into the open learning materials short assignments or exercises to be handed in during lecture time.** This can help to ensure that learners keep up with the intended pace. Sometimes you could actually take in their work and mark it, or take it in just to check how the materials were working, then return it to the class for peer-marking or self-marking.

8    **Get learners to use the open learning materials as a framework for their lecture notes.** For example, use some lecture time for learners to do particular tasks around information that is already in their open learning materials. This conditions them to bring the materials to the large-group sessions, and increases the probability that they will have worked on them before the session. It also allows you to set additional follow-up tasks during the session.

9    **Turn some lectures into tutorials.** For example, choose particular areas for students to learn with the open learning materials, and arrange a follow-up lecture slot that will be devoted to questions and discussion about the material, rather than introducing anything further on such occasions.

10 **Turn some lectures into large-group, interactive learning experiences.** Interactive handouts can be designed for large-group sessions, where the handouts themselves are in effect miniature open learning packages, including stated learning outcomes, tasks and feedback responses. Such large-group sessions not only build upon the principles of learning by doing and learning from feedback, but they also help learners themselves to develop approaches which they can extend to working with fully fledged open learning packages.

11 **Explain how, and when, the open learning material content will be assessed.** It can be useful to stage some of the assessment somewhat earlier than the end of the course or module, so that some face-to-face time can be reserved for feedback to the class about any significant problems that were found with the part of the curriculum delivered by open learning.

12 **Consider using computer-delivered assessment for appropriate parts of the material.** Such assessment can be based on a bank of questions, with each learner being given a random selection from the bank on the occasion when they take a test. The tests can be done either in a booked computer laboratory (with invigilation, if necessary, to minimize possibilities of cheating), or could be networked over a week or two when the purpose of the assessment may be primarily formative. The use of passwords can add to the security of the tests, and the reporting software can save you a considerable amount of time and avoid you having to do tasks such as marking and making class score lists manually.

# 11

# Which learners are particularly helped?

All sorts of people use open learning in distance learning mode. The following categories of learners are included as those who can be particularly helped in different ways. Many parallels may also be drawn to the use of flexible learning elements in college-based programmes, where similar benefits can be delivered to a variety of constituencies of the student population.

1   **High fliers.** Very able learners are often frustrated or bored by traditional class-based programmes, as the pace is normally made to suit the average learner and may be much too slow for high fliers. With open learning, they can speed through the parts they already know, or the topics they find easy and straightforward. They can work through a package concentrating only on the parts that are new to them, or which they find sufficiently challenging.

2   **Low fliers.** The least able learners in a group are often disadvantaged when the pace of delivery of traditional programmes is too fast for them. They can be embarrassed in class situations by being seen not to know things, or unable to do tasks that their fellow learners have no difficulty with. With open learning, they can take their time and practise until they have mastered things. They have the opportunity to spend much longer than other learners may take.

3   **Anxious learners.** Some people are easily embarrassed if they get things wrong, especially when they are seen to make mistakes. With open learning, they have the opportunity to learn from making mistakes in the comfort of privacy, as they try self-assessment questions and exercises, and learn from the feedback responses accompanying such components of an interactive learning package.

4    **Learners with a particular block.** Learners who have a particular problem with an important component of a course can benefit from open learning, in that they can work as often as they wish through materials designed to give them practice in the topic concerned. It can be useful to incorporate self-assessment exercises, with detailed feedback specially included for those learners who have problems with the topic.

5    **Learners needing to make up an identified shortfall.** For example, in science and engineering programmes, it is often found quite suddenly that some learners in a group have not got particular maths skills. Rather than hold up the progress of a whole class, self-study components can be issued to those students who need to get up to speed in the areas involved. When the learners have a sense of ownership of the need that these materials will address, they make best use of the materials.

6    **People learning in a second language.** In class situations, such learners are disadvantaged in that they may be spending much of their energy simply making sense of the words with little time left to make sense of the ideas and concepts. With open learning materials, they can work through them at their own pace with the aid of a dictionary, or with the help of students already fluent in the language in which the materials are written.

7    **Part-time learners.** These are often people with many competing pressures on their time, or with irregular opportunities for studying, perhaps due to shift work, work away from home or uneven demands being normal in their jobs. Open learning materials allow them to manage their studying effectively, and to make the most of those periods where they have more time to study.

8    **People who don't like being taught!** Surprisingly, such people are found in college-based courses, but there are many more of these who would not consider going to an educational institution. Open learning allows such people to have a much greater degree of autonomy and ownership of their studies.

9    **Learners who only want to do part of the whole.** Some learners may only want – or need – to achieve a few carefully selected learning outcomes that are relevant to their work or even to their leisure activities. With an open learning package, they are in a position to select those parts they want to study, whereas in face-to-face courses they may have to wait quite some time before the parts they are really interested in are covered.

10   **Learners with special needs.** For example, people with limited mobility may find it hard to get to the venue of a traditional course, but may have few problems when studying at home. Learners with other problems may be able to work through open learning materials with the aid of an appropriate helper or supporter. Open and flexible learning is increasingly being used to address the particular needs of diverse groups including carers, prisoners, mentally-ill people, religious groups, socially excluded people, and so on.

# Chapter 2   Adopt, adapt or start from scratch?

12   Adopt, adapt or start from scratch?
13   Establishing the learning quality of published materials
14   Establishing the content relevance of published materials
15   What to look for in computer-based materials
16   Planning how to adopt
17   Planning how to adapt

This chapter is essentially about value for money. When resource constraints are tight, it may seem that open or flexible learning can stretch human resources further. It may seem sensible to package up some elements of the curriculum, stop teaching them traditionally and replace them with open learning. However, the time taken to conceive, develop, pilot and refine an open learning package is almost always underestimated. This is why in this chapter I am encouraging you to explore the potential benefits of adopting existing learning resource materials if they will serve your purposes and meet your students' needs. However, buying in off-the-shelf materials has its own resource implications, and it becomes crucially important to choose wisely.

An intermediate position is to start with published or commercially available learning materials, and to adapt them both to suit your own teaching style and to meet the particular subject-related needs of your students, as well as to meet their approaches to learning.

Therefore, it seems necessary to encourage colleagues to make some time to search for and evaluate existing learning resource materials. Materials which could be adapted to flexible learning usage are not necessarily fully fledged interactive open learning packages, and could be anything from a good textbook to a collection of journal articles that have worked well as handouts with a lecture group. In such cases, the *content* of an open learning resource does not have to be developed from scratch, but the *process* side of making it work flexibly may need to be done from cold. This could be achieved by writing a study guide to the existing resource material, rather than adapting it. It takes *far* less time to write an effective study guide to support existing resource materials than to develop a new open learning package. I have, however, left my suggestions about writing study guides until the end of the *next* chapter, so that you can see how a good one should aim to capture all of the features which make a good open learning package work well.

Meanwhile, I would like you to use the present chapter to explore whether you really *need* to compose new open learning materials, and to develop your skills at looking critically at what already exists, so that you are in a more informed position to decide whether to adopt, adapt or start from scratch.

# 12

# Adopt, adapt or start from scratch?

A vast amount of material has been written to support open and flexible learning. Some of this material looks good, but does not work. Some looks bad but does work. The following questions and suggestions offer some help towards reaching a logical decision about some of the factors involved in deciding whether to embark on creating new flexible learning resource materials, or to prepare to adopt or adapt existing materials.

1   **Do you really want to start from scratch?** If your answer is a definite 'yes', this is probably a good enough reason for at least exploring in more depth the implications of creating new flexible learning materials. If the answer is a definite 'no', it is probably worth your while to look carefully at some of the possibilities there may be of adopting existing materials, or adapting them to meet the needs of your particular open learners.

2   **Have you got time to start from scratch?** As should be clear from many parts of this book, designing open learning materials is a time consuming activity, and usually takes quite a lot longer than is planned! In particular, materials need to be piloted and adjusted on the basis of feedback from learners (and tutors, mentors and anyone else who sees how they work in practice), and such piloting should be done quite extensively well before the materials are committed to their first 'published' form or made generally available. Starting from scratch can be really expensive if starting from a position of inexperience too.

3    **Do you actually need to start from scratch?** Many institutions have developed their own policies, approaches and housestyles relating to the production and support of open and flexible learning, and have staff development and training provision available. Such policies and training are often centrally resourced in the institution, and project management support may also be available. Before being tempted to start out on your own, it is important to make sure that you have checked out where your institution stands.

4    **Have you got the skills to start from scratch?** If you have already developed highly successful open learning materials, you will not be in any doubt about your answer to this question. If, however, you have not yet gone up the learning curve involved in such development, you may not realize the diversity of skills that are involved.

5    **Will you be a lone spirit, or a member of a cohesive team?** While it is indeed possible for one person to create and design an excellent open learning resource, the statistical probability of this happening is much less than when a committed team tackles the task. Members of such a team need to have broad agreement on the nature of most of the hallmarks of effective open learning materials, as well as time to work together on developing open learning alongside all the other things that they may be doing.

6    **Will the right people be doing it for the right reasons?** When creating new open learning materials, everyone involved needs to believe in what they are doing, not just you! Team membership should not be dictated by who happens to have some slack in their timetable, or even by an identified need to establish a flexible learning pathway in a topic taught by particular people.

7    **Have you got the resources to start from scratch?** Creating new open learning materials involves more than skilled writers, who know both the subject involved and the problems that students have in learning it. Other things to consider include layout, production, reproduction, print-runs, design of media-based elements, administration, communication to students learning independently, monitoring student progress and the design and implementation of related assessment elements.

8    **Are you in a position to find out what exists already?** There is a wealth of published open learning material, increasingly accessible through catalogues and databases. There is an even greater wealth of material that is unpublished, but working effectively locally in colleges, universities, training organizations and elsewhere. There is no easy way

of tracking down some of this material or of finding out how useful or relevant some of it may be to the needs of your own students. Most colleges have staff such as Learning Resources Managers, and links to consortia, whereby progress can be made in tracking down and evaluating suitable resource materials.

9    **Are you in a position to make informed judgements on the quality of existing published resources?** This is not just a matter of checking that the subject matter is correct, up to date and relevant to the needs of your learners. It is about being able to interrogate the materials on how well they support your students' learning and how well they integrate with other parts of their curriculum.

10   **Are you in a position to buy in identified suitable resources?** Almost anything that exists can be purchased for use in your own institution, but the cost-benefit analysis needs to be considered carefully. Detailed negotiations may need to be undertaken with the owners of the copyright of the work concerned, if you intend to mass reproduce it. Site licences for local reproduction may need to be negotiated. Bulk discounts may be an option when purchasing ready-to-use materials from elsewhere.

11   **How important may the 'not invented here syndrome' be?** One of the biggest problems with adopting other people's materials is that the sense of ownership is lost. This may be reflected by a lack of trust in the materials. Reactions such as, 'it's not the way I would have covered this topic' or, 'this just isn't at the right level for my learners' or, 'this misses out some important points my learners need to address' reflect genuine problems.

# 13

# Establishing the learning quality of published materials

One of the problems with commercially available open learning materials is that some look good but just do not work, and others work well, but do not look attractive. Much published material falls between these two positions. What really matters is that the materials cause your open learners to learn successfully, but acceptable standards of appearance and style remain on the agenda. The following checklist may be a useful start when reviewing existing published materials, while exploring the possibility of adopting them or adapting them for your own open learners. Interrogate the materials on the following aspects of open learning quality.

1   **Look first at the intended learning outcomes.** If these are well expressed, and in language that your learners will be able to understand easily, the materials are off to a good start in your interrogation. It is also desirable that the learning outcomes are written in a personal, involving way, so that your open learners will feel that the materials are directly suitable for them.

2   **Check how interactive the materials are.** There should be learning-by-doing opportunities throughout the materials. This is better than just having a collection of self-assessment questions or activities at the end of each section or module. Check whether the tasks and exercises are pitched at an appropriate level, so that they could give your learners useful practice and the chance to learn from anticipated mistakes.

3   **Check how well the materials respond to open learners.** Look particularly at the responses to self-assessment questions. These should be considerably more than simply answers to the questions. Your learners should be able to find out not only whether their own attempts at the questions were successful or not, but should also be able to find out easily from the responses what might have gone wrong with their own attempts when unsuccessful.

4    **Check the standards.** The standards to which the learning outcomes will be delivered should be most clearly evident from the levels of tasks in the materials. In particular, if tutor-marked assignment questions are included in the materials, see whether they are pitched at an appropriate level for your learners, and decide whether you could use them as they stand.

5    **Think about the tone and style of the materials.** Most open learning materials work better when the tone and style is relatively personal and informal. The materials should be involving, with learners addressed as 'you', and when appropriate the authors talking to learners as 'I'. Check, however, that the tone will not be found patronising by your open learners. This is not necessarily the same as whether *you* may find the tone or style too informal – remember that you are not *learning* from the materials.

6    **Think about the ownership issues.** For example, if the materials are designed for learners to write all over them – filling in answers to questions, entering calculations, sketching diagrams, and so on – learners are likely to get a high degree of ownership of their learning from the materials. If the materials are more like textbooks, this ownership may be reduced, and learners may not regard the materials as primary learning resources.

7    **Think ahead to what you may wish to add to the materials.** For example, when materials do not yet contain sufficient self-assessment questions, or when feedback responses are not yet self-sufficient enough for your learners, you may well be able to bridge the gap by adding questions and responses of your own. This can be well worth doing if there are other aspects of the materials that make them particularly attractive as a starting point for your own fine tuning.

8    **Look at the layout and structure of the materials.** For open learners to trust them, the materials should look professional and credible. They should be able to find their way easily backwards as well as forwards through the materials. There should be good signposting, showing how each section of the materials fits in to the whole, and linking the intended learning outcomes to the tasks and activities in the materials.

9    **See whether you can get feedback on how well the materials actually work.** Check whether there are other colleges or organizations already using the materials, and try to find out how well they are doing their job there. Reputable sources of published open learning materials will normally be only too pleased to provide details of major clients.

10 **Check the costs involved.** There are different ways of 'adopting' open learning materials. These range from purchasing copies in the numbers you require for your own open learners to acquiring a site licence to reproduce your own copies. If you are dealing with a minority specialist option, the economics will probably favour buying copies directly. Bulk discounts may be available for significant purchases, and it can be worth buying in supplies to last for more than one 'run' of the materials, but this should only be considered when you are really certain that these are the materials that you want to use.

# 14

# Establishing the content relevance of published materials

In the previous set of suggestions we looked at some questions with which to interrogate the *learning* quality of published open learning materials. Next, we explore some further important questions aiming to help you to establish the degree of relevance of the *content* of the materials to your own open learning programmes. It is important that enough time is devoted to checking out the content of materials, and that such time is made available to those with this responsibility, or that someone appropriate is commissioned to evaluate the materials.

1   **Check carefully the match between the published learning outcomes, and those of your own programme.** It is normal to expect some differences. Some of your own learning outcomes may be absent from the published materials. The materials may at times go well beyond your own learning outcomes. It is important to establish what fraction of the published materials will be directly relevant to your own open learning programme. If it is less than half, this is normally a signal to continue searching elsewhere.

2   **Check that the published materials are compatible with other parts of your learners' studies.** For example, check that they use subject specific conventions or approaches that will be familiar to your own learners.

3   **Seek out reviews of the learning materials.** Just as with textbooks, reviews can help you make decisions about which to adopt and which to reject, and reviews of open learning materials can be useful indicators of their quality. Reviews tend to concentrate more on the subject matter than the ways that the materials actually deliver successful learning, and are therefore useful in the context of establishing relevance.

4    **Decide whether the materials are sufficiently up to date.** A quick way to do this is to look for references to 'further reading', or tasks briefing learners to make use of other reference books or articles on the topics covered. You will normally know of the most respected source materials and any recent developments which should be encompassed within the open learning materials, or referred to in them.

5    **Check that any resources that the materials depend upon are available.** For example, if the open learning materials are written with one or more set textbooks or articles to be used alongside them, make sure that these materials are still available. Even important set texts go out of print, often between editions, and the next edition may not lend itself to the particular tasks for which it was referred to in the open learning materials.

6    **Check the relevance of the learning-by-doing tasks in the materials.** Compare these with the sorts of tasks you would set students in conventional courses at the same level. Watch particularly for tasks which could be considered too basic, or 'missing the point' of important elements of learning. Also look out for tasks that may be too advanced and which may stop your open learners in their tracks.

7    **Estimate the expected time which learners may need to spend using the materials.** There are often indications of this built in to open learning materials, but you may need to work out upper and lower limits that would reasonably relate to your own least able and most able learners. Match these timescales to the overall duration (or equivalent duration) of your open learning programme, and the relative importance of the topics addressed by the materials. For example, if a published workbook is expected to take the average open learner 12 hours to work through, but the topic concerned is only one-tenth of your 60-hour equivalent module, you may need to look for a more concise package covering the same ground.

8    **Check that you can live with the ways the materials address important topics.** This includes equal opportunities approaches, for example, check how the materials portray male/female roles in the content of case studies and illustrations. Do not get into the 'not invented here syndrome'. If you really do not like the way the materials handle an important concept, you are probably well advised to look for other materials. Any distrust or reservations you have about learning materials may be quite infectious, and your learners may quickly pick up doubts about the materials and lose their confidence to learn from them.

9   **Work out how much you may need to add to the materials.** It is quite
    normal for published materials not to cover everything that you would if
    you were designing them yourself. It is relatively easy to bridge small
    gaps by designing handouts or small workbooks to address them.

10  **Work out how much you might wish to delete!** You do not want your
    open learners to waste their time or energy by doing things in published
    materials which are not connected to the learning outcomes of their own
    programmes, or which are not involved in their own assessment in some
    way. It is perfectly feasible to brief your learners on such lines as, 'Don't
    do anything with Section 9 unless you want to just for your own interest;
    it's not on your agenda.' To decide which published materials you may
    wish to adopt, make sure that there is not too much in this category.

# 15

# What to look for in computer-based materials

Much of the foregoing discussion about interrogating published print-based open learning materials can readily be extended to computer-based materials. For example, many of the questions about how well the materials will support flexible learning continue to apply, and the issues of whether the material is authoritative and up to date, are still present. The following additional suggestions may help you to select suitable computer-based resource materials to support open learning programmes.

1   **Remember that it is harder to get a good idea of the effectiveness of computer-based materials than for paper-based ones.** This is not least because it is not possible to flick through the whole of a computer-based package in the same way as is possible with a printed package. It can be quite hard to get a feel for the overall shape of the learning that is intended to accompany a computer-based package.

2   **The best first step to evaluate a computer-based package is to work through it yourself.** You may need to remind yourself that you probably know a lot more about the content than your open learners will. At the same time, many open learners are likely to be more competent at finding their way round computer-based materials than their teachers or trainers.

3   **Prepare your own checklist to interrogate computer-based materials.** Decide the questions that you need to ask about each possible package, before committing yourself to purchase. Questions could include:

   • Are the materials supplied with workbook elements?

   • Do students themselves *need* these elements?

   • Can support materials be freely photocopied?

   • What is the standard of the equipment needed to run the packages effectively?

- What level of technical support and backup will be required?
- Does the software include individual student progress monitoring and tracking?
- Do the materials make good use of pre-test and post-test features?
- Can the materials run effectively on a network?
- Are there licensing implications if you wish to run the package on more than one machine?
- Can you afford multiple copies if the materials are multimedia, single access packages?

4   **Check the stated intended learning outcomes.** Most computer-based packages either present these on-screen towards the beginning of the programme, or specify them in accompanying documentation or workbooks. One danger is that such documentation often becomes separated from the actual terminal or computer, and learners may be entirely dependent on what they see on-screen to set the scene for what they are about to study.

5   **Try to establish the pedigree of the software.** Some computer-based packages have been thoroughly tested and developed, and have been updated and revised several times since their launch. Such packages normally give some details of the history of their development. Beware of packages, however well presented, that have been published or disseminated without real trialling.

6   **Look at how the medium is used to enhance learning.** If the material does no more than to present on glass what could have been presented equally well on paper, it is probably not worth investigating further. The medium should do something that helps learning, such as causing learners to engage in interaction that they may have skipped if the same tasks or questions were set in print.

7   **Try to *watch* a small group of target-group learners work with the package.** This gives you a better idea of how long you can expect students to need to spend with the package. More importantly, listening to the things learners say to each other gives you valuable clues about any further help or support that may be needed for future open learners working through the same package on their own.

8   **Do your own trialling with learners working on their own.** Devise ways of measuring the extent to which working through the package helped them achieve *your* intended learning outcomes. If possible, measure the added value that the package delivered to them, by testing before and after use of the package.

9 **Try to find out what else computer-based packages teach your learners.** While the intended learning outcomes may be topic specific, students often learn equally valuable skills relating to learning from computer-based materials in general.

10 **Try to measure your open learners' retention of their learning.** With computer-based materials, learners' achievements may be high immediately after their work with the package, but may fade quite rapidly afterwards. Even when they still have the opportunity to revisit a computer-based package for revision, they may not do so as readily as they would revise from paper-based resources or their own notes.

11 **Think ahead to how you could enhance the use of a good package.** For example, consider getting learners to work through a package, combined with very short but fairly frequent tutor-marked questions or exercises presented on-screen. This can be achieved using e-mail to provide communication to a tutor, and feedback from the tutor. It is then possible to gain ongoing evidence of learners' successes and failures while they learn from computer-based materials. They are also more likely to work through the package more slowly and systematically if from time to time their learning is interrogated by tutor-marked elements.

# 16

# Planning how to adopt

In previous sets of suggestions, we explored some of the questions with which to interrogate published resource materials, when exploring the feasibility of adopting them as they stand, or adapting them, for use in your own open learning programmes. Below are some practical suggestions about how to adopt materials that you have found to be suitable.

1  **Work out whether learners will be issued with their own personal copies.** Will learners be able to keep their copies after they have finished working through them? If not, will there be a problem about learners writing answers to self-assessment questions on the materials? It is obviously best where learners can retain learning resource materials, as they can then relearn from them later when necessary. Is it feasible to offer a purchase or loan option to learners themselves? If the materials are to be issued on a loan basis, how will you be able to get them back? What percentage can you expect to get back in a fit state for reissue? How many 'runs' may the materials survive?

2  **Work out how many copies of the materials you will need.** This will normally be rather more than the open learners you expect in your first cohort. Even so, it can be quite difficult to estimate the number of copies to purchase, especially if your planning is for more than a single year. Explore with the owners or providers of the materials the purchase options available to you. Look at the economies of scale that may be achieved by bulk purchases, or by obtaining a site licence for reproduction of the materials.

3  **Check out delivery dates firmly.** It is most unsatisfactory, if at least the first parts of the materials you have chosen are not available at the start of your open learners' studies. Similarly, if the materials are bulky, you may not have space to store multiple copies for a long period of time.

4    **Take particular care with computer-based materials.** Something you have seen working well on someone else's network may not work on your hardware. There may be bugs to iron out. There may be incompatibility problems with other software, or with printers, modems and so on. Almost all such difficulties are solvable, but sometimes solutions take time. Get the computer-based elements up and running well before your open learners may need them.

5    **Protect at least one full copy of everything!** You never know when you will need that last available copy for an important purpose. The assignment booklet may be needed, for example, to show teaching quality assessors or external examiners the level of the work expected from students. The installation instructions for computer software may be needed again when your system has to be cleared of a virus and programs need to be reinstalled. Keep all the essential papers and data in a safe place, and file them well so everyone knows what is there.

6    **Work out exactly how you intend your open learners to make use of the adopted materials.** Work out how long they can expect to spend with each element of these materials. Clarify which intended learning outcomes are most relevant to them. Prioritize which tasks and exercises they should regard as central, and which as optional.

7    **Revisit the intended learning outcomes.** You may need to restate these, fitting them in to the context of the overall outcomes your open learners are working towards. You may need to prioritize the published outcomes in the purchased materials, helping your learners to see which ones are central, and which are more peripheral.

8    **Think ahead to how you will assess the learning outcomes.** Work out what proportion of the overall assessment will be linked to learning achieved through using the materials. Maybe start straightaway on designing tutor-marked assessment questions and related exam questions. Perhaps also design some indicative sample questions which you can give out to learners along with the materials, so they can see the standards they are expected to reach in their achievement of the outcomes. Double check that there are no unpleasant surprises for learners due to differences between indicative questions and real assessments.

9    **Compose briefing instructions for your open learners.** Introduce the adopted materials, explaining where they fit in to the overall learning programme. If necessary, write short notes explaining any differences between the approaches used in the materials and in other resources they may be working with.

10    **Think about study skills advice.** It can be particularly helpful to open
        learners to have tailored suggestions for 'how to get the most out of...'
        both for print-based materials and computer-based ones. Such briefings
        can also suggest additional ways that learners can make opportunities to
        practise the most important things you intend them to learn using the
        materials.

# 17

# Planning how to adapt

Adapting existing open learning materials happens more frequently than adopting them as they stand. It is, not surprisingly, rare that someone else's package is exactly appropriate for your own learners. If you are adapting published materials for use by your learners, you will need to think about most of the suggestions I made in my earlier set about 'Deciding how to adopt'. Moreover, there will be the adaptations themselves to think about. Although this task may seem daunting, it becomes more manageable if broken down into the elements described below.

1   **Regard adaptation positively.** It is a lot of work adapting an open learning package to make it directly meet the needs of your learners, in the context of their overall study programme. However, there are benefits for you, too. For a start, you will feel a stronger sense of ownership of the materials after you have done your work with them, than if you had used them in their original state. There is also the possibility that in future you may be in a position to think about co-publishing your adaptation, with the authors of the original materials, especially if the added value that your adaptations bring to them proves to be very significant.

2   **Start with the intended learning outcomes.** If these are published within the package, rank them in terms of which are essential, which are desirable but not central, and which are optional for your own open learners. Then look carefully for anything important that is missed in the published outcomes. Look for outcomes that have not been stated, but that could be achieved using the materials as they stand. Then look for outcomes that are not covered by the materials, as these will become the focus of some of your adaptations.

3   **Think early about other resource materials you may intend your learners to use, alongside the adapted ones.** For example, there may be sections of textbooks, handouts you already use, or key articles that you would prefer them to work from than from parts of the materials you are adapting. Start clarifying in your own mind the parts of the materials that you are adapting that you *do not* want your open learners to work through.

4   **Look carefully at the interactive elements.** Examine the learning that occurs through the self-assessment questions, exercises and activities. Decide which of these are really useful, as they stand, for your own learners. Aim to keep these as they are. Then start looking for intended learning outcomes that are not yet matched by opportunities for learning by doing, and draft out further self-assessment questions and tasks as necessary. Adding such interaction is normally the most important stage in adapting materials for your own purposes.

5   **Look at the quality of the responses to self-assessment questions and activities.** The feedback that learners receive after engaging with the interactive elements is crucial for their learning. You may well decide to recompose the feedback components for a significant proportion of the self-assessment questions, particularly those you have already identified as central to the learning outcomes.

6   **Think about adding some completely new self-assessment questions and feedback responses.** Consider how much practice your own open learners may need to make sense of the most important ideas, concepts and procedures covered by the learning materials. It is better to have too many good interactive elements, and then to whittle them down to realistic amounts, than to have a too restricted range at the outset.

7   **Review any tutor-marked assignments already in the materials.** You may well want to change these, fine tuning them so that the tutor-marked agenda fits in with other such elements in different parts of your open learners' overall programme. You may be able to use tutor-marked assignments that you already use in face-to-face programmes instead.

8   **Consider writing a commentary to talk your open learners right through the materials as they use them.** This could be in a small booklet that they keep alongside them as they work through the materials. It is useful to use this as a guided tour through the materials. Specific comments such as 'I suggest you skip the exercise on p.34 unless you had a problem with the question on p.30', or 'only aim to remember the 3 most important factors listed on p.51' can be very helpful to your learners.

9 **Think about whether to do a 'cut-and-paste' job on the package being adapted.** Whether you can do this may depend upon the conditions on which you purchased or licensed your use of the package. However, it is worth, if necessary, negotiating with the authors or owners of the copyright of the material that you are adapting. A cut-and-paste job begins to become a preferred option when the changes, additions and deletions you decide to make reach more than a third of the original material. Be particularly careful, however, not to infringe copyright legislation regarding the material from the original package which remains intact.

10 **Plan a careful pilot of your adaptation.** It is quite likely that after the first 'run' you will wish to make substantial further adaptations, not least to the parts that you introduced yourself to the package. Beware of going into production of large numbers of copies of Adaptation Version 1. Even though it is more economical to do fairly large reprographic runs, it is false economy if you end up binning a lot of copies of a version that you have to change further.

# Chapter 3    Writing open learning materials

18    Making profiles of your open learners
19    Tone and style for open learning
20    Choosing an efficient strategy
21    Defining intended learning outcomes
22    Expressing competences
23    Writing self-assessment questions
24    Writing feedback responses to structured questions
25    Writing multiple-choice questions
26    Writing feedback responses to multiple-choice questions
27    Writing open-ended questions and responses
28    Writing an introduction which works
29    Finishing well: reviews and summaries
30    Writing study guides

Although this chapter is entitled 'Writing open learning materials', this should not be taken to mean that it is *only* about writing fully fledged, stand alone open learning packages from scratch. Indeed, I have tried to include in this chapter suggestions to help you at each important step on the way to such a venture, but each part of the chapter is just as relevant to *adapting* existing resource materials for flexible learning usage.

I start the chapter by encouraging you to make profiles of some typical target-group learners. This suggestion also applies if you find yourself providing tutorial support for students working in flexible learning mode. Having some clear pictures of likely learners in mind makes it much easier to put pen to paper (whether creating or adapting) to write the main elements which add up to an open learning package.

Choosing an appropriate tone and style for open learning materials is important, both when writing new packages and adapting or editing existing ones. It is now broadly accepted that for open learning materials to be found accessible and user-friendly by learners, the tone should be considerably less formal than in some traditional resources such as textbooks or journal articles. The interactive elements and study skills guidance need to be user-friendly, but this does not preclude case-study material and subject content exposition from using a more formal approach, and illustrating the standard of language which students should be able to handle in the context of their studies and at the level of complexity concerned.

The next section offers advice on choices of strategy for putting together open learning materials, aiming to help you to save time and energy by focusing your writing (or adapting) on the most important elements. For example, designing and expressing intended learning outcomes, and writing self-assessment questions and feedback responses, are much more crucial to the success of open learning materials than merely expounding the subject material.

The next two sections are on spelling out to learners exactly what you intend the learning materials to do for them. Whether we call these objectives or competence frameworks, they should set out the agenda clearly for learners. Furthermore, the objectives or intended learning outcomes should become the basis upon which learners' achievements are in due course measured and assessed.

The next sections provide suggestions on the design of self-assessment questions and feedback responses. This should be done iteratively, making adjustments to questions and responses in turn, until the responses provide self-sufficient help for learners who have attempted the questions, whether or not their attempts have been successful. Next, the same principles are applied to one of the most important question types: multiple-choice. Open-ended questions are considerably more difficult to respond to, but can play valuable roles in bridging the gap between structured formative self-assessment questions, and tutor-marked summative assessments.

I continue this chapter with some suggestions about writing introductions to open learning materials. There is no second chance to make a good first impression on open learners. The introduction can be make or break in determining their motivation and their attitude to the material which follows. It is best to postpone writing the final version of the introduction until the material which follows has not only been written, but also piloted.

I conclude this chapter with some suggestions about writing study guides, to lead open learners through directed usage of existing resources such as textbooks, journal articles and so on. Although the task of writing a study guide is much smaller in scale than writing self-standing open learning materials, the skills needed include all of those introduced earlier in the chapter, as it will normally be necessary to express intended learning outcomes, and create learning-by-doing in the form of self-assessment questions, and provide feedback to learners' efforts, in just the same ways as in a self-standing package.

# 18

# Making profiles of your open learners

In some ways, I *should* have put this advice in the section about tutor support, rather than here! However, it is as important for writers to think about their target audience as it is for tutors to think about their students. Whether you are starting to draft new open learning materials, or preparing to use or adapt existing resource materials to implement a new open learning pathway or programme, it is useful to step back and remind yourself about the sorts of *people* your learners actually are. The following suggestions may help you to build up profiles of your target-group learners, and help you to design or support open learning that will work well for them.

1   **Think of at least three people who could be open learners on your programme.** Base one or two of these on any actual experience you have of the sorts of people you have known as open learners, but make one of them someone quite different – someone who may have particular expectations or needs as an open learner.

2   **If possible, work with a group of colleagues in making your profiles.** While you can go a long way on your own, it is particularly enriching to work with a course team on the suggestions which are presented below, comparing and contrasting your individual answers to each question, and gaining a fuller picture of the constituencies of learners who may actually participate in your planned programme.

3   **Give each imaginary learner a name and an age.** Make these suitably different, to reflect the age range that you could reasonably anticipate, and the gender and ethnic factors that could be important to underpin your planning to deliver an effective open learning experience to all participants on your programme.

4   **Write down two or three reasons why each learner may be taking your programme.** Make these as diverse as they are likely to be in real life. Some will *want* to learn, some will *need* to learn, some may have been *told* to learn, and so on. Think about the real ownership of these reasons for studying, and how this may affect each learner's motivation and commitment.

5   **Write down two or three reasons why they will be studying by *open* learning.** These could include that they are not able to be released from work to attend a traditional programme, or that there is no such programme in their area, or that they *prefer* the idea of open learning, and so on. Be creative, do not just stick to these reasons!

6   **Jot down some keywords for each learner about the strengths they may bring to open learning.** For example, some may already have highly developed learning skills through past education or training, others may have a significant head start in the subjects involved, and so on. It is important to continue to bear in mind the differing starting points when developing a programme for open learners.

7   **Jot down some weaknesses and anxieties that could affect the progress of each of your imaginary learners.** Some may have chips on their shoulders from previous experience (maybe in the distant past) of education or training. Some may have anxieties about this new and different way of learning. Some may be anxious about the prospect of tutor-assessment. In practice, you can expect to continue to be surprised at the diversity of experience (and hangups) that people bring to open learning.

8   **Think ahead to what their expectations may be regarding tutor support.** What kinds of help (reasonable and unreasonable) may they believe that they can expect from their tutors? How may this affect the tone and style of tutor feedback which will work best for them?

9   **Think of other factors in their lives which will impinge on their open learning.** Try to sketch out real life circumstances for each learner. Think of the effects of their employment (if employed), or their other studies (if students), their social life, family, friends, hobbies and interests.

10  **Try to identify the hazards which could stop them in their tracks.** Probably the biggest danger with open learning is non-completion rather than failure. For each imaginary learner, work out the triggers or combinations of circumstances which could cause them to give up. Try to decide how you could monitor such circumstances so that there would be someone to help them or encourage them at these critical times.

11   **Consider turning your profiles into a case-study booklet.** Where a group of colleagues have all addressed the questions and issues above, it can be useful to make a booklet of one learner per page, starting with names and ages, and capturing the diversity of the possible constituencies of open learners. Later, with real learners, these case studies can become a frame of reference, and can be a shorthand form of talking about situations and problems. 'Janice seems to be in the "Tanya" situation at present' can be a quick way of describing a situation to the group.

12   **Develop the profiles further on the basis of actual open learners.** Using information from tutors, or from feedback questionnaires completed by learners, further *real* information can be gathered to enrich the case-study booklet. It may be important to make at least some of this information duly anonymous, as learners sometimes may not wish to have their names traced to the situations that they have given information about.

# 19

# Tone and style for open learning

Whether writing new open learning materials, adapting existing resources, or writing study guide elements to support students working with learning resource materials, the tone and style of your writing may need to be different from that which you would use for other purposes. One of the principal differences between material designed for open learning and textbooks, journals and manuals, is that open learning material is considered best when written in an accessible, user-friendly style. The following suggestions should help you to pitch your level of informality appropriately and avoid your learners being intimidated or patronized.

1   **Remember that you are 'talking' to people.** They may well be working alone while reading your materials. Remind yourself of the sorts of people that you anticipate them to be, and try to write in a way which will capture their interest, gain their involvement and motivate them to learn actively from your materials.

2   **Think about what your students find comfortable to read.** Find out what kinds of magazines and newspapers they prefer. Look at the tone and style of the writing in these materials. Academics are often surprised at the simplicity of style of skilled journalists, who can be describing complex situations, but using simple language structures.

3   **Remember that you have not got tone of voice, facial expression or emphasis to help you out.** The words you choose need to be able to convey as many as possible of the more subtle nuances that you would unconsciously use in speech.

4　**Think carefully about how to address them.** The most natural way is to talk to them as 'you'. This is preferable to talking about 'students', 'learners', 'trainees' or even subject-specific terms such as 'accountants', 'managers', and so on. Everyone is 'you'! It is, however, often useful to mention other labels in such contexts as, 'One of the biggest problems accountants have with… is…' or, 'students who have not met the concept of… will find a useful source is…'

5　**Be particularly careful to make task briefings and instructions personal.** This is where the use of 'you' is most helpful. In self-assessment questions, tutor-marked assignments and any other occasions where you want your learners to do something, they are less likely to skip the task if there is at least one 'you' in your briefing.

6　**Try to make the material itself involving.** There is an abundance of third-person passive material in textbooks, journal articles and maybe in the reference materials you are briefing your open learners to work with. The briefings or adaptations *you* are writing are the most important parts for your learners, so try to ensure that they get the most out of them by feeling involved and included.

7　**Think about who the author is.** It is normally best, when appropriate, to refer to yourself as 'I' in briefings, instructions and explanations. Phrases such as, 'I found the best way into this was to…' and, 'I think you will find it helpful to…' do much to keep your learners' attention and to make them feel less lonely, even when working alone.

8　**Be careful with 'we'.** This is a particular problem when you may be co-authoring your open learning materials (or study guides) with other people. Then it seems natural to write 'we', but it sometimes does not come across as sincerely as you intend it to. In such cases it may be worthwhile thinking about occasionally slipping in phrases such as 'Both of the authors found that when we tried to…'

9　**Use short words when possible.** The meaning of a sentence is much more likely to get across unambiguously if you avoid unnecessary long words. This is particularly important with briefings for tasks, exercises and assignments. You may well *need* to use long words relating to the subject you are writing about, if your learners are expected to use them too, but check that there is a genuine purpose every time you use a long or unusual word or phrase. There is a tendency in academic writing to demonstrate one's sophistication in the application of linguistics, sometimes to the detriment of the intended message that is to be communicated. Some writers seem to be under the misapprehension that if anyone can understand their writing without having to pause to consolidate each idea in turn, they must be failing to reach the standard required. The preceding two sentences in this tip are meant to illustrate the point!

10   **Keep sentences as short as you can.** This is most crucial when difficult ideas or concepts are involved, or when giving briefings to self-assessment questions, tasks, exercises or tutor-marked assignments. People are much more likely to make assumptions, possibly dangerous ones, about long sentences than about shorter ones. Even when writing *about* topics where long sentences are part of the discipline (for example, law or sociology) it is important to keep *your* sentences short, and leave the lengthier ones for the subject matter extracts themselves.

11   **Think about contractions.** In everyday speech, most of us use contractions such as 'I've', 'let's', 'you'll', 'we've', 'it's' and so on. Some people, unfortunately, regard such language as sloppy. Make your own decision as to whether your students will learn better from material that presents ideas in an informal way.

12   **Watch your punctuation.** A series of ideas separated by commas in a long sentence is more difficult to grasp than a list of bullet points. With such a list, readers can immediately see how many factors are involved, rather than having to count them up along the length of a sentence.

13   **Ask rather than tell.** The question mark key is probably the most powerful one on your keyboard when it comes to helping people to think rather than just to read. Asking a question brings the chance for learners to think about their own answers before reading yours.

14   **Don't overuse exclamation marks!** They lose their impact if used too often. While you may mean to convey a wry smile with such a device, if your readers have already become irritated by the frequency with which they occur in your writing, they will prove counterproductive. Try just deleting them, and see if your point still comes across. The first one in this tip is not necessary!

15   **Test out your tone by listening to it.** Consider getting someone to tape-record an extract of your open learning writing. Then sit back and listen. Any problems someone else had reading it into the recorder, or problems you have in hearing what you meant to write, may help you to see how you could adjust your style.

16   **Use the sentence starter 'what I *really* mean is...'** Saying this to yourself before writing a sentence often means that what you write comes across rather better than it otherwise might have done. Imagine your reader asking 'so what?' and respond to this too, maybe in your next sentence.

# 20

# Choosing an efficient strategy

The most difficult stage in starting out to design an open learning resource can be working out a logical and efficient order in which to approach the separate tasks involved. These suggestions should help you to avoid wasting too much time, and particularly aim to help to ensure that the work you do is directly related to composing learning material, rather than writing out yet another textbook. These suggestions provide headlines to many of the aspects of open learning which are covered in much more detail later in this book. I suggest that you return to this agenda frequently to check that your approach remains focused and efficient.

1   **Think again!** Before really getting started on designing open learning resource material, it is worth looking back, and asking yourself a few basic questions once more. These include:

   • Am I the best person to write this material?

   • Is there a materials production unit in my institution which can help me?

   • Are there any experienced materials editors there whose expertise I can depend upon?

   • Is there graphics design help and support?

   • Is there already an institutional housestyle?

   • Can someone else produce the open learning materials, while I simply supply the raw material and notes on how I want it to work in open learning mode?

   If after asking these questions, you decide to press ahead with designing your own materials, the following steps should save you some time and energy.

2   **Don't just start writing subject material.** An open learning package is much more than just the subject matter it contains, and is something for learners to *do* rather than just something to read.

3   **Get the feel of your target audience.** The better you know the sorts of people who will be your learners, the easier it is to write for them. It is worth spending some time on the suggestions earlier in this book about making profiles of the main groups which will make up your target audience.

4   **Express your intended learning outcomes.** It is worth making a skeleton of the topics that your material will cover in the form of learning outcomes, at least in draft form, before writing anything else. You may wish to draft your learning outcomes in the format of a competence framework. Having established the learning outcomes, you are in a much better position to ensure that the content of your open learning material will be developed in a coherent and logical order.

5   **Seek feedback on your draft learning outcomes.** Check that they are seen by colleagues to be at the right level for the material you are designing. In particular, check that they make sense to members of your target audience of learners, and are clear and unambiguous to them.

6   **Design questions, tasks and activities firmly based on your intended learning outcomes.** Some of the outcomes may require several tasks and activities to cover them. It is also useful to plan in draft form activities that will span two or three learning outcomes simultaneously, to help pave the way towards integrating your package and linking the outcomes to each other.

7   **Test your draft questions, tasks and activities.** These will in due course be the basis of the learning-by-doing in your package, and will set the scene for the feedback responses you will design. It is extremely useful to test these questions and tasks first, with anyone you can get to try them out, particularly with students who may be close to your anticipated target audience. Finding out their most common mistakes and difficulties paves the way towards the design of useful feedback responses, and helps you adjust the wording of the tasks to avoid ambiguity or confusion.

8   **Plan your feedback responses.** Decide how best you will let your learners know how well, or how badly, they have done in their attempts at each of your tasks, activities and questions.

9   **Think ahead to assessment.** Work out which of the questions, tasks and activities you have designed will be useful as self-assessment exercises, where feedback responses can be provided to learners in print in the learning package, or on-screen if you are designing a computer-based package. Work out which exercises need the skills of a tutor to respond to them, and will usefully become components of tutor-marked assignments.

10   **Map out your questions, tasks and activities into a logical sequence.** Along with the matching learning outcomes, this provides you with a strong skeleton on which to proceed to flesh out the content of your open learning material.

11   **Work out your main headings and subheadings.** It is wise to base these firmly on the things that your learners are going to be doing, reflecting the learning outcomes you have devised. This is much better than devising headings purely on the basis of the subjects and topics covered, or on the original syllabus you may have started out with.

12   **Write 'bridges'.** Most of these will lead from the feedback response you have written for one question, task or activity into the next activity that your learners will meet. Sometimes these bridges will need to provide new information to set the scene for the next activity. It is important to ensure that these bridges are as short and relevant as you can make them, and that they do not run off on tangents to the main agenda provided by the skeleton you have already made. This also ensures that you make your writing really efficient, and save your valuable time.

13   **Write the introductions last.** The best time to write any introduction is when you know exactly what you are introducing. It is much easier to lead in to the first question, task or activity when you know how it (and the feedback associated with it) fits in to the material as a whole, and you know how and why you have arranged the sequence of activities in the way you have already devised. Although you may need to write draft introductions when first putting together your package for piloting, it is really useful to revisit these after testing out how learners get on with the activities and feedback responses, and to include in the final version of each introduction suggestions to learners about how to approach the material that follows, based on what was learnt from piloting.

# 21

# Defining intended learning outcomes

The intended learning outcomes are the most important starting-point for any teaching–learning programme, and are particularly important when writing open learning materials. The learning outcomes can be expressed in terms of the objectives which learners should be able to *show* that they have achieved. The following suggestions address the design of such outcomes in general terms, while the next set of suggestions provides some specific advice on using competence frameworks to express such outcomes.

1   **Write your learning outcomes in plain English.** Remind yourself for whom you are writing them! It is much more friendly to write outcomes along the lines, 'when you've worked through this package, you will be able to...' than to state, 'the expected learning outcomes of this section are that the student will...'

2   **Take care when the curriculum is already defined.** There may already be externally defined learning outcomes, or they may have been set down some time ago when the course or programme was validated, but these may be written in language which is not user-friendly for students, and which is more connected with the teaching of the subject than the learning process. You may need to translate these outcomes, so that they will be more useful to your learners.

3   **Your intended learning outcomes should serve as a map to your open learning materials.** Students and others will look at the outcomes to see if the materials are going to be relevant to their needs or intentions. The level and standards associated with your material will be judged by reference to the stated learning outcomes.

4    **Don't promise what you can't deliver.** It is tempting to design learning outcomes that seem to be the answers to everyone's dreams. However, the real test for your material will be whether it is seen to allow learners to achieve the outcomes. It is important to be able to link each learning outcome to an assessable activity or assignment.

5    **Focus on the intended performance of your learners.** Think in terms of the ways that they will be able to demonstrate their achievements when they have successfully worked through your package. It can be helpful to think of the kinds of evidence that your learners may accumulate to demonstrate their performance.

6    **Avoid using words such as 'understand' or 'know' in your outcomes.** While it may be intended that learners will in due course know things and understand things, these are not sufficiently clear as learning outcome statements. Work out instead what you wish your learners to be able to *do* to demonstrate their knowledge or understanding

7    **Don't start at the beginning.** It is often much harder to write the outcomes that will be associated with the beginning of a package, and it is best to leave attempting this until you have got into your stride regarding writing outcomes. In addition, it is often much easier to work out what the 'early' outcomes actually should be once you have established where these outcomes are leading learners towards.

8    **Think ahead to assessment.** A well-designed set of learning outcomes should automatically become a firm framework for the design of assessed tasks. It is worth asking yourself 'How can I measure this?' for each draft learning outcome. If it is easy to think of how it will be measured, you can normally go ahead and design the outcome. If it is much harder to think of how it could be measured, it is usually a signal that you may need to think further about the outcome, and try to relate it more firmly to tangible evidence that could be assessed.

9    **Think about implications for prerequisite knowledge or skills.** These too can be described in terms of the learning outcomes associated with them, for example as descriptions of the outcomes which learners should already be in a position to demonstrate, to show them that they are ready to start work on your package.

10   **Ask yourself for each learning outcome, 'why do they need to become able to achieve this?'** Wherever you can, fine tune the wording of your learning outcomes to help your learners to see the *purpose* of each outcome.

11   **Keep sentences short.** It is important that your learners will be able to get the gist of each learning outcome without having to reread them several times, or ponder on what they really mean.

12   **Consider illustrating your outcomes with 'for example...' descriptions.** If necessary, such extra details could be added in smaller print, or in brackets, or in another colour. Such additional detail can be invaluable to learners in giving them a better idea about what their achievement of the outcomes may actually amount to in practice.

13   **Test-run your learning outcome statements.** Ask target audience learners 'what do you think this really means?' to check that your intentions are being communicated clearly to learners. Also, test your outcomes statements out on colleagues, and ask them whether you have missed anything important, or whether they can suggest any changes to your wording.

# 22

# Expressing competences

This is a particular way of expressing learning outcomes, and using them as the basis for the design of teaching, learning and assessment. The suggestions made in the previous section continue to apply, and the additional tips below may help you to maximize the effectiveness of a competence-based approach for your open learning package, if you find yourself required to adopt such a format.

1   **Check what may already have been done.** With competence-based frameworks being used widely (for example, National Vocational Qualifications in the UK), it is possible that you may not need to devise a completely new set of competences for your learning package, but may be able to adopt or adapt work that has already been done. In any case, existing specifications may still leave you free to design open learning to concentrate on activities, evidence collection by learners, and the underpinning knowledge needed to support and inform their learning.

2   **Feel free to re-express any existing competence frameworks that you may use as your starting point.** Many existing frameworks are quite impersonal and bureaucratic in the tone of the language used to express learning outcomes, and you may well wish to think carefully about the wording in the context of your own open learning development.

3   **Start by working out the elements of competence that you wish your learners to achieve.** These are normally expressed as 'can do...' statements, summarising the principal behaviours that your learners will be expected to become able to demonstrate.

4   **Work out any prerequisite competences and express these in the same way.** It can be useful to your learners if they can tell fairly easily whether they are already in a position to start working with your material, or whether there are shortfalls they should address before starting.

5   **Write performance criteria for each element of competence.** You may be able to adapt these from existing criteria if you are starting with a framework that has already been devised. These criteria should give detail of the actual things that learners should be able to do to demonstrate that they have achieved each competence element, and the criteria provide the basis for assessment of learners' competences.

6   **Decide how you are going to give further detail about standards.** It is normal to devise 'range statements' associated with each performance criterion, to show the standard or extent of the work that learners need to do to demonstrate their achievement. Such further detail is provided in some competence-based frameworks, such as National Vocational Qualifications specifications in the UK.

7   **Express 'evidence descriptors'.** These complete the competence framework, by giving illustrations of the kinds of evidence which learners should collect, to demonstrate that they have achieved each element of competence to the standards indicated by the performance criteria along with the range statements. In practice, the evidence descriptors usually mean more to learners than the rest of the framework, and it is often useful to start one's explanation of a particular element of competence with an illustration of the sorts of evidence that may be involved.

8   **Think about the links with assessment.** The competence framework should provide a thorough basis for any assessment associated with your open learning material. There should be no unpleasant surprises for learners, such as an assessment task relating to something that has not been covered by the framework.

9   **Work backwards from assessment too.** If you already know of important things which need to be included in the assessment associated with your open learning material, check that they are covered by the competence framework, and add additional detail as necessary to the elements of competence, range statements, performance criteria and evidence descriptors until such assessments are fully included in the framework.

10  **Check out that all the wording of your competence framework is understandable by your target learners.** Follow through the suggestions made in the previous section to help you to make adjustments and clarifications to the wording of your competence framework.

# 23

# Writing self-assessment questions

Self-assessment questions, activities and exercises are one of the most important features of open learning materials, as they allow learning by doing through practising, and also provide valuable opportunities for learning by trial and error. It is normally safer to use structured question formats, rather than open-ended ones for self-assessment questions, as it is then much more possible to respond to exactly what your open learners *do* with each task. We will look separately at the use of one particular structured question format: multiple-choice, and how best to respond to these. However, it is also possible, with care, to include some open-ended self-assessment tasks too, providing you know how you will help your learners to self-assess their own answers. The following suggestions may help you to ensure that the self-assessment exercises you design are serving your learners well.

1   **Write lots of them!** Writing self-assessment questions gets quicker and easier with practice. Like most things, it is learnt best by doing it.

2   **Make good use of existing materials.** If you are already teaching the topic concerned, you are likely to have accumulated quite a stock of class exercises, homework assignments, practice questions and so on. Many of these will lend themselves to being translated into self-assessment questions and feedback responses.

3   **Look at as many samples of open learning material as you can.** This helps you see a variety of types and styles, and enriches your own writing of self-assessment components. Look at the examples you see from the learner's point of view. In particular, look at the kinds of question where you feel that you are getting useful feedback if you make mistakes or do not actually choose the best or correct option in multiple-choice formats. Look for those types of question where you do not know why you made a mistake – and avoid writing questions of these sorts.

4   **Keep your intended learning outcomes firmly in mind.** These should provide the agenda for all of the questions, tasks and activities that you set in your open learning material. If you find yourself tempted to use a question or exercise that is not directly related to the learning outcomes, check whether it would be a good idea to add new learning outcomes to your agenda to link such a question into your material properly.

5   **Keep your tutor-marked assessment ideas firmly in mind.** Learners who successfully work through all of your self-assessment questions, exercises and activities should be able to expect confidently that they will succeed in any other kinds of assessment they will encounter. The self-assessment components should provide them with all the practice they reasonably need, as well as allowing them to learn from mistakes in the comfort of privacy, before mistakes count against them.

6   **Work out exactly what each question is intended to test.** There needs to be a good answer to: 'what's this question for?' Sometimes the answer will be to allow learners to confirm that they have mastered an idea, and at other times it may be to alert them to something that they may have a problem with. It is important that learners do not view the self-assessment questions as trivial – they may not even attempt them then.

7   **Don't test too many things at once.** It is usually best to keep self-assessment tasks relatively straightforward and not too complex. This makes it much easier to design feedback responses, addressing anticipated problems that learners may have found.

8   **Have a feedback response in mind.** To work as a self-assessment activity, it has to be possible to respond to what your learners actually do with it. This usually means that you will need to structure your questions carefully, so that you can *know* what your learners are likely to do with them, and respond appropriately to learners who succeed, and to learners who do not.

9   **Use a variety of structured questions.** For example, with multiple-choice questions you can respond directly, and differently, to learners choosing different distracters (wrong or less good options), and to learners who choose the correct or best option (the 'key').

10  **Don't just use multiple-choice formats.** While these are very versatile, it can become tedious for learners if this is the only kind of self-assessment question they meet. Ring the changes. Try some prioritising or sequencing questions, where you ask your learners to put given things in the best order of priority or the most logical sequence. Try some completion or

filling blanks questions, to help your learners see whether or not they know what words should be added to complete the sense of sentences, definitions, or statements.

11 **Consider the use of at least some open-ended tasks as self-assessment questions.** While you cannot guarantee to be able to respond to exactly what your open learners may have done with open-ended questions, there are ways of helping them to self-assess their own answers to these. The biggest danger is that learners are quite likely not to go to the trouble to critically assess their own answers, unless you make the self-assessment part of the exercise really valuable – and interesting – to them. For this reason, I have included later in this book a separate set of suggestions about responding to open-ended questions.

12 **Try your questions out on learners (and anyone else!)** The best way of finding out whether a question, task or activity will make a good self-assessment exercise is to see how people get on with it. You will find that this helps a great deal when you come to write the feedback responses, as you will be much more aware of the sorts of things that learners may do incorrectly, or the most likely errors that they could make.

13 **Discard lots of self-assessment questions.** Having gone to the trouble of designing self-assessment components, it is tempting to leave them in your materials even when you know from piloting and testing them that they are not too effective. It is better to start with a large number of possible questions, and select only those which work well. You can always recycle the discarded ones for usage in other contexts in which they will work better, such as in class questions or tutorial exercises.

# 24

# Writing feedback responses to structured questions

The self-assessment questions and exercises provide open learners with opportunities to learn by doing, practising and making mistakes in the comfort of privacy. To capitalize on all the effort that goes into designing such tasks, learners need to be given really useful feedback every time they have a go at a self-assessed exercise. It is considerably easier to write feedback responses to structured questions than to open-ended tasks, as it is known to at least some extent the kinds of answers which open learners are likely to have given. The following suggestions should help you to ensure that feedback is playing an optimal role in your students' learning from structured questions in open learning materials.

1   **Check that you can actually respond to what learners have done with each structured self-assessment question.** If you cannot actually be fairly sure about the various possibilities, it probably will not work as a structured self-assessment question.

2   **Responses should be much more than just the answers to the questions.** Thousands of textbooks come with questions and answers for students to work through; few students make good use of these, and the students who do engage with such questions are probably those who would be most likely to succeed in any case. In open learning materials, feedback responses are particularly important for those learners who *need* some feedback on what they have done in their attempts at structured self-assessment questions – usually because the questions have helped to show them where their learning is not yet complete.

3   **Regard the responses to self-assessment tasks as the most important measure of the quality of your open learning materials.** It is such responses that make the most important difference between open learning materials and textbooks. Most people reviewing the quality of open

learning materials turn straight to the responses to structured self-assessment questions. If these responses are really *responding* to learners, rather than just giving the answers to the questions, the quality of the material as a whole is likely to be regarded as high.

4   **Ensure that each response addresses the learners' question, 'Was I right?'.** Sometimes questions and tasks lend themselves to right and wrong answers. On other occasions there may be no right answer, but your feedback responses will still need to give learners a frame of reference with which to judge the quality of their own attempts.

5   **Cater carefully for learners who get things wrong.** When they get something wrong, there are two further questions they want answers to, 'What *is* the right (or best) answer?' and, 'Why wasn't I right?' It is the latter of these two questions that is the most important for you to address through your feedback comments. It is not always enough to be pointed in the direction of the correct or preferred answer. Learners want to know how their own answers (or choices of option) measure up and what, if anything, they may have got confused about or wrong in their attempts at the question.

6   **Don't forget to praise good answers or choices.** Learners who have attempted any self-assessment task successfully deserve a word or two of praise. But do not just say 'well done' every time; this gets very boring! Also do not use superlatives such as 'splendid' except for the few tasks where learners really deserve an accolade when successful. Milder forms of praise such as 'that's right…' or 'yes indeed…' have their place for responses to things that most learners should be handling successfully.

7   **Give messages of sympathy for learners who may be feeling daunted.** When it is expected that many learners will make a particular mistake, it makes a great deal of difference to them if they read such phrases in your responses as, 'Don't worry, most people have trouble with this idea at first' or, 'This was actually quite a hard question.'

8   **Give the good (or bad) news straightaway.** As soon as learners have attempted a self-assessment exercise they want to know how they have done. It is very frustrating for them if they have to read through a rambling explanation before they begin to work out whether they did well or badly. Start the response crisply with the news. For example, when responding to a multiple-choice question it can be helpful to open with 'The best choice is Option C'. This gives all learners quick feedback on the basic issue of whether their choice was the preferred option.

9    **Start each part of your response with the verdict.** For example, if responding to a true–false question, remind your learners along the following lines, 'It is *false* to say that…' so that they know *that* it was false, and *what* exactly was false from the outset of your response. You can then elaborate and explain *why* it was false.

10   **Make the responses worth reading.** If learners just glance at your responses, or ignore them altogether, they are not getting the benefit of the feedback that you have planned for them. It can be a useful tactic to include at least some important ideas *only* in your feedback responses, and to refer in your main text to the fact that this is where the information is located. Simply making the responses interesting and lively helps to ensure that they are used as intended by your learners.

11   **Don't make mountains out of molehills!** Avoid the temptation to predict, and respond to, every possible thing that your open learners could do with your self-assessment questions. Learners should be able to absorb your feedback to most questions within a few minutes.

# 25

# Writing multiple-choice questions

One format of self-assessment question which can work particularly well in open learning materials is multiple-choice. The greatest advantage of these is that (when well designed) they can provide appropriate feedback to open learners whether or not they make correct (or best) selections from the options offered to them. A multiple-choice question has three main ingredients: the 'stem' setting the context, the 'key' which is the best option or the correct one, and 'distractors' – options containing faults or errors. The following suggestions should help you to get all three parts of multiple-choice questions working effectively.

1   **Make sure that the key is definitely correct.** It should not be possible for students to find anything wrong or arguable in the key. It is often the most able students who spot something wrong with the key, and this can be frustrating to them when they see a response which does not acknowledge the level of thinking they exercised.

2   **Make sure that the key does not stand out for the wrong reasons as being correct.** The key should not be given away by containing leading wording from the stem, nor should it be of significantly different length than the other options. Also make sure that any grammar links between the stem and the key do not give the key away. You may think such matters would rarely arise, but the last person to spot them is usually the author of the question!

3   **Take care with 'definites' versus 'indefinites'.** It is all right to have sets of options including indefinite words such as 'sometimes, often, usually, rarely' or sets of definite words such as 'always, never, all, none' but it is not wise to combine the two kinds of words in a given question, as the indefinite options are more likely to be chosen as correct by anyone who is just guessing – and are probably correct, too!

4   **Make sure that the stem provides a clear task.** For example, be clear about whether 'which …?' means 'which *one*…?', or 'which (one or more) …?' There is no harm in asking 'which *two* of the following…?' when you really want learners to pick two options, and are going to respond accordingly in your feedback.

5   **Avoid options which may let your learners think too little.** It is best to avoid options such as 'all of these' or 'none of these'. These tend to be chosen as cop out selections by learners who are not thinking deeply enough to identify the best option. Having expressed this reservation, either of these options can be valuable if used *occasionally* where you really want to make a point about 'all of these' or 'none of these' being the best answer.

6   **Be careful with negative questions.** For example, if asking, 'which one of the following is *not* true?' or, 'which is an *exception* to the rule?' make it really stand out that it is a 'wrong' option that has to be selected in such questions; candidates become accustomed to looking for correct options.

7   **Make sure that there is something wrong with each distractor.** Remember that when you write a feedback response to a distractor you need to be able to explain convincingly what is wrong with it, or why the key is better.

8   **Choose distractors which represent likely errors.** There is no point in having distractors which are not chosen as 'correct' by at least someone. Distractors need to be as plausible as you can make them. That said, it is fine to inject a note of humour occasionally by using an 'unlikely' distractor!

9   **Let students help you to find better distractors.** It is worth posing the stem as an open-ended question in a face-to-face class if you have such an opportunity, and finding out what the most common wrong answers are. These can then form the basis of your distractors.

10  **Try questions out on a large group if you can.** For example, in a lecture put the question up on the screen, and ask for a show of hands for each option in turn. When everyone chooses the correct (or best) option, your distractors may need to be made a bit more appealing! If you do not have the chance to work with large groups of learners, it is still worth trying out your questions on as many people as you can, even if one at a time and at a distance (or electronically).

11   **Remember that multiple-choice questions are not restricted to simple formats.** For example, an extended set of options can be used, with the question asking students to decide which *combination* of options is correct or best (for example 'a, d, e' or 'b, c, e' and so on). Browse through some open learning materials to explore the range of multiple-choice formats that is possible. For example, the Science Foundation Course of the Open University in the UK has many excellent examples of sophisticated (and difficult) multiple-choice questions.

# 26

# Writing feedback responses to multiple-choice questions

Whatever form your multiple-choice questions take (print, computer-based, or test), open learners want (and need) to find out two things every time they make a choice: 'Was I right?' and 'if not, *why* not'. The following suggestions may help your responses provide useful, quick feedback to learners.

1   **Think about when your response will be seen.** For example, learners may see your response immediately on-screen after picking an option in a computer-based package, or at the back of a print-based package in the self-assessment question responses, or they may see it in print after completing a series of questions in a multiple-choice test.

2   **Make it immediately clear whether the option was correct or not.** Instant feedback can be very useful, particularly when you can remind students of why they were right, or show them why they were wrong. Even if your open learners receive the response somewhat later, their first priority will still be to establish whether their choice was successful.

3   **Give appropriate praise for the choice of correct options.** A few well chosen words can be encouraging for learners who made the correct choice.

4   **Make sure that 'well done' messages don't get boring or out of control!** There are hundreds of ways of responding 'well done'. Save the 'splendid' responses for right answers to really tricky questions. Milder forms of 'well done' include 'yes', 'right', 'of course', and so on.

5    **Respond to learners who choose distractors.** It is of little use just saying to them, 'wrong, the correct option was A'. Learners want (and need) to find out *why* the distractor was not the best option. If you cannot respond to a distractor, take it as a sign that it was not a good distractor in the first place. Good distractors are wrong for a reason, not just wrong!

6    **Acknowledge learners who choose options that are partly correct.** When part of a distractor is correct, use words to remind learners who have chosen it that they did indeed have some good reasons for their choices. For example: 'while it is true to say that…, however it is not true to conclude that…'

7    **Let open learners who choose distractors off the hook gently.** They may well be working on their own, so do not leave them feeling that they must be the only people ever to have made such mistakes. Words like 'this was a tricky question', or 'most people find this hard at first' can go a long way towards making it more acceptable to choose distractors. This can also help to build open learners trust in the value of making mistakes in the comfort of privacy, then finding out why.

8    **Give learners the opportunity to give you feedback on your feedback.** Check particularly that when you explain what was wrong with distractors that learners get your messages clearly. Ask your open learners to mark onto their materials any feedback responses which they cannot understand. Often the understanding will be about to dawn, and slowing down to identify exactly what it is that is not yet understood is all it takes to put things right. When this does not happen, it could be that the fault lies in the question or in the feedback, and some editing may be needed for the next edition.

9    **Think of visual ways of responding.** Some learners may wish to be responded to visually rather than with words – at least sometimes. Try to arrange coffee with a computer-graphics expert if you are designing responses for a computer-based package.

10   **Keep the language of responses familiar and friendly.** Responses should address the student as 'you' and should use simple, accessible vocabulary. A sense of humour usually helps, but excessive humour (especially feeble puns) can be counter-productive!

# 27

# Writing open-ended questions and responses

It is much harder to write feedback responses to open-ended questions. In particular, you cannot be certain what your learners have done in answer to the questions, you can only guess. In general, open-ended questions serve a more useful role in tutor-marked assignments, when human judgement and comment can be used to respond to learners' answers. The following suggestions, however, may help you to include at least some open-ended questions in the self-assessed parts of your open learning materials. In the first few suggestions, I concentrate on ways of turning open-ended questions into ones which have at least some degree of self-assessment potential, then I end with some suggestions for open-ended tasks which are more to do with getting learners to reflect on their own studies.

1   **Have a good reason each time you decide to use an open-ended self-assessment question.** In other words, do not just use open-ended questions because they are much easier to set! The best place for open-ended questions is normally tutor-marked assignments, where human response can be available to whatever interpretations open learners place on the meaning of the questions.

2   **Include a few open-ended self-assessment questions as 'dry runs' for tutor-marked components.** Some open learners can be quite anxious about tutor-marked assessment. It may be some years since they have had authoritative feedback on their written work. Giving them some practice at writing out more extended answers can help increase their confidence, and can illustrate the standard of answers which may be expected from them. To make best use of these 'dry-runs', learners need to write down their own answers to the open-ended questions, *then* self-assess their own answers using guidance notes and marking criteria provided in their learning materials. These may need to be 'hidden' away from the questions, so that learners really have the chance to answer the questions themselves before seeing on what basis to self-assess their answers.

3   **Include open-ended questions as a means of helping open learners discover much more about the assessment criteria which will be used in tutor-marked elements.** Such questions can be used with the self-assessment dimension as their main purpose, with detailed briefings about how learners should evaluate and mark their own answers.

4   **Use open-ended questions to extend the comfort of privacy to free-form answers.** One of the advantages of structured self-assessment questions is the opportunity they provide for open learners to learn from their mistakes in the comfort of privacy. This dimension can be extended to open-ended questions, especially when you have a good idea of the possible kinds of mistakes which you want to bring to the attention of your open learners.

5   **Make the questions, and your responses, as interesting as you can.** Open-ended questions will normally take your learners a lot more time to attempt than structured questions, and the temptation to skip open-ended self-assessment questions is always there. If the task looks fascinating and important, this temptation is reduced.

6   **Explain *why* you are setting each open-ended self-assessment question.** For example, flag them as dry runs for tutor-marked assignments, or practice for typical exam questions and so on, with the real purpose of helping your learners to see *what counts* in their answers, and to find out about how the assessment criteria will work in practice.

7   **Compose feedback responses carefully.** Work out exactly what you want your open learners to *do* to self-assess their answers. Give detailed briefings about how they should go through their answers, including what to look for in them that would score marks, or that would lose marks in a formally-assessed answer.

8   **Consider getting open learners to apply a 'real' marking scheme to their own answers.** You could base the marking scheme on one that is tried and tested from a previous exam or assignment, and where you already know the most likely difficulties and areas of weakness. You will almost certainly have to recompose the marking scheme in learner-friendly language, however.

9   **Think about the value of model answers.** These are not in themselves sufficient as responses to open-ended self-assessment questions, but can be part of an illustration of what is really being looked for in terms of standard and content of answers. Model answers work best as feedback to learners when they are accompanied by a commentary (maybe in a separate column down the right-hand side of the model answers).

10    **Think about the possibilities of responding to open-ended questions on audiotape.** For extended open-ended tasks, it can be useful to talk open learners through their own work, by recording a short audiotape which helps them go about self-assessing their work. The benefits of this include tone of voice, emphasis, and the fact that learners can be briefed to stop the tape and do something with their own answers, then restart the tape and continue. Such usage of audiotape can be particularly useful for *any* self-assessment questions, and also for tutor-marked assignments, where learners are studying in a second language. Audiotape also comes into its own as a feedback medium for partially sighted learners.

11    **Bear in mind that it may not be possible to respond completely.** Open-ended self-assessment questions are unlikely to be entirely self-assessable, even with model answers and marking schemes. The self-assessment only goes as far as learners' own comparisons of their answers with the response framework provided in the materials. It is useful to legitimize follow-up face-to-face or e-mail discussions with tutors, for learners who may still have problems self-assessing their own answers to such questions.

12    **Consider using some completely open-ended questions.** For example, it can be productive to ask open learners to make entries in their own personal learning logs or reflective journals or diaries. Think of designing specific questions as the basis for such reflection and consolidation. It could be that learners' answers are not assessed at all, or alternatively you could set a tutor-marked assignment question asking learners to process further some of the thinking they may have done for open-ended questions of this sort.

# 28

# Writing an introduction which works

The importance of the first page or two in an open learning package (or the first few screens in a computer-based one) can not be overestimated. Your learners' attitudes are formed by the first few minutes they spend with your materials. The following suggestions may help you to get them off to a successful start.

1   **Beware of trying to start at the beginning.** The problem is that to start most things at the beginning takes you so far back that most people already know most of it, and become bored by reading it. You may well have to backtrack to make sure that each learner can make sense of the starting point, but choose something more important to be the focus of your attitude forming introduction.

2   **Use the introduction to explain how the package will work best.** It can be useful to explain any conventions used in the package, and to let learners know in advance about any equipment or other resources they will need to have available as they work further into the package.

3   **Start as you mean to go on.** If you are writing in an informal, friendly style in the body of your material, do not preface it all by an impersonal stolid introduction. It is worth capturing your learners' interest right from the start. Also, this means that they will not be 'thrown' by a sudden switch to a less formal approach when you start to involve them in self-assessment questions and other activities.

4   **Don't write the introduction too early.** The best time to write the introduction (or the final version of it) is when you know everything towards which it is leading. When you know exactly what is in your package or study guide, and *how* the material is designed to work, you are in a much better position to write an introduction to the learning package, and not just to the topic concerned.

5    **Think twice about calling it 'Introduction'.** There is something about the word that implies for many people 'this is not really important, it's only a lead-in, and I can skip it'. In its own way, use your introduction to address the question 'so what?', which may be in the minds of at least some of your learners.

6    **Don't try to introduce too much at once.** Even when you know the whole of what will follow, it is usually best to lead into only a manageable amount of it. Remember that you will have many more lead-in sections throughout the material.

7    **Ask yourself: 'what does this introduction actually do?'** Think about turning your answer to this into a question-heading. See if you can use this to explain to your learners *why* it will be worth their while to look at it carefully. For example, 'Why is thermodynamics important?' will work better than 'An introduction to basic thermodynamics'.

8    **Consider breaking your introduction up into separate elements.** When there is more than one purpose to be served by your introduction, work out the objectives it will serve, and maybe pose these in the very first part of it, then deal with each under a different, appropriate sub-heading.

9    **Consider making your introduction interactive.** Starting with a setting-the-scene task, or a 'find out how much you already know' quiz, can be a good way of getting your open learners involved right from the start. It can be useful to start with a pre-test or diagnostic test, particularly if prior knowledge of something in particular will be important later in the material. It is, however, important not to make pre-tests too intimidating, and to introduce them in a way where you make it clear that your learners are not *expected* to answer all the questions correctly.

10   **Seek particular feedback on drafts of your introduction.** Ask colleagues and learners alike how they *feel* about the introduction. Ask them whether you are taking anything for granted, and perhaps need to add a sentence here and there to clarify matters. Consider asking someone else to draft an introduction for you (with or without sight of yours), and see whether they come up with something about which you may otherwise not have thought.

11   **Don't expect your introduction to be remembered by your learners.** For example, even when you make important points in your introduction, such as about how best to make use of the learning materials, your learners will probably not return to the introduction again. You may well need to reinforce or repeat important points at various stages throughout your materials.

# 29

# Finishing well: reviews and summaries

As with most kinds of creative writing, to generate a good impression an open learning package should not just fizzle out. Introductions may be your one chance to make a good *first* impression, but how the package ends makes important *last* impressions. The following suggestions may help you decide how best to bring your open learning materials to a successful, robust conclusion.

1  **Design your conclusions as a revision aid.** A well-designed set of conclusions should be a useful reminder of the main things you intend your learners to be able to do, or to know, when they have completed their work on your package.

2  **When you think you've reached the end, don't feel you have to ramble on.** It sometimes takes some courage to decide to end. If you put off the moment of coming to a conclusion for too long, you are almost certain to be losing your learners' interest.

3  **Plan your ending quite early.** It helps to know where you are heading towards, to marshal your arguments and tidy up any loose ends as you get nearer to your conclusions. It is sometimes quite difficult to decide exactly where to finish, and it often helps to aim towards ending with a particularly important point or idea.

4  **If you write 'Conclusions', make them short.** Learners often look at conclusions while working through materials, and sometimes before starting, to check out the destination towards which they are working. For this to work well, it is best if the conclusions are no more than half a page in text-based materials, or one screen in computer-based ones. Whatever form your conclusions take, try to end with a short sentence, which is likely to have more impact than a long one.

5   **Beware of saying 'well done'.** This can work with computer-based materials, where to reach the final screen you *know* that each learner has worked through all of the package. In print-based materials, learners can look at the conclusions at any time, and seeing 'well done' is somewhat artificial, especially if they have not yet done any real work on the package. 'Well done' messages are probably best reserved for responses to self-assessment questions, for example to learners who have chosen the correct (or best) option in multiple-choice tasks.

6   **Check that your conclusions have a close relationship with the intended learning outcomes.** If there is any discrepancy here, it could be that you need to go back and adjust the intended learning outcomes.

7   **Use conclusions to point forwards as well as to look back.** If the materials are a stepping-stone towards further packages, it can be useful to explain briefly those that follow on most directly from the present one. It can be helpful in such cases to give your learners a little advice along the lines 'the one thing from this package that you will most need for the next one is...'

8   **Think of ways of ending with an activity.** Think about the merits of a test yourself quiz, or a rate yourself exercise against the intended learning outcomes. Try not to *end* the whole package with an exercise, however, without some form of wrapping up and summarizing the main content first.

9   **Consider ending with a short feedback questionnaire.** This in its own way flags the end of the material. Remember to thank your respondents in advance for their feedback; this helps to ensure that you will receive their feedback! Use at least part of the questionnaire to cause your learners to think back through some of their learning. For example, ask them which self-assessment question response they found most valuable in terms of feedback, or ask them to prioritize half-a-dozen topics in terms of most difficult to least difficult.

10  **Think about the last thing in your package.** This may not in fact be your conclusions, due to the structure of the materials. For example, in print-based materials, the responses to the self-assessment questions could be at the end of the package. There may also be appendices such as a glossary, an index, or some supplementary, remedial or optional information about an earlier part of the package. You may still want to have something at the very end of the package that carries a sense of completion. In such cases, one option is to consider repeating the intended learning outcomes this time phrased, 'now that you have completed your work on this package, check that you can...'

# 30

# Writing study guides

Sometimes the quickest, and perhaps best, way to implement an open learning pathway is to collect and organize some relatively traditional materials, and to write a study guide to take students through them in a planned, structured way. Study guides are particularly useful for academic subjects where it may be necessary to get students to review a lot of case-study or research-based material. Writing study guide material involves many of the processes considered already in this chapter, but it is also important to think carefully about how students are briefed to use the traditional resources. The following suggestions should help you to ensure that your study guide helps students to make the most of such resources.

1  **Make each study guide attractive and motivating.** The study guide may be the central document that open learners work with all of the time on your module, while they refer from it to different books, articles, videos and multimedia resources. Explain to students how the study guide is intended to help them balance the various activities that they will do in their studies.

2  **Link the intended learning outcomes to the resources.** For example, when different textbooks or articles contain the reference material for your students' learning, it helps to indicate which learning outcome is addressed in each different resource material.

3  **Link self-assessment questions to the respective resources.** One of the most important components of an effective study guide is the interaction which plays the same part as self-assessment questions and feedback responses in self-standing open learning materials. With study guide materials, the subject matter is likely to be located in supporting texts or articles, and it helps to specify which source material(s) should best be used by open learners when working on the questions.

4 **Link feedback responses to the respective resources.** Rather than write out detailed feedback responses, it is often possible to refer students to particular sections or paragraphs in their resource materials. However, it remains best to write the main response feedback, and to confine such references to 'further explanation' or 'see also the discussion in…'

5 **Don't refer students to large amounts of material at once.** For example, suggesting that open learners should read Chapter 4 of a textbook is not likely to cause them to learn much from their reading. It is better to brief them to focus their reading on particular pages or sections, and to legitimize the process of merely scanning less relevant or less important material.

6 **Use the study guide to suggest reasonable timescales.** For example, when referring to textbooks or computer-based learning packages, it can be useful to give your learners a rough idea of the maximum and minimum times you expect them to spend with each source. This can help your learners to avoid becoming sidetracked and, for example, spending too much time working with one particular source.

7 **Give learners an agenda *before* they read extracts from other resources.** For example, suggest that 'you should read Chapter 3, Sections 3.3–3.5 next, looking for answers to the following five questions…' When students have already got questions in their minds, their reading becomes considerably more active, and when they discover some information which answers one of their questions, they tend to learn it more successfully.

8 **Advise learners on what *not* to read.** One of the problems with using external sources, such as textbooks, is that there is usually a significant amount of such sources which is not directly relevant to the intended learning outcomes of the open learning module. It can be helpful to advise students along the lines 'There is no need for you to look at Chapters 4–5 of this source, unless you happen to be particularly interested in the content; this will not relate to any assessments in the present programme'. Most open learners are quick to take such hints!

9 **Consider setting tasks that cause learners to compare and contrast different sources.** When the same topic is addressed in different ways in respective sources, rather than gloss over the difference, it can be valuable for students to make their own minds up about which approach they like best. Compare and contrast tasks may be better as part of tutor-marked assignments than as self-assessment exercises, as tutor feedback may add further value to students' own decisions about the different approaches they encounter.

10   **Include study skills help.** Writing a good study guide is about helping students with the *processes* they should aim to use to make the most of the resources with which they are working. It can be useful to have a separate commentary, including practicable suggestions about how to approach working with each different source or resource.

# Chapter 4   Communications and information technologies

31   Using video for open learning
32   Using audiotapes for open learning
33   Using computer-based open learning packages
34   Using e-mail to support open learning
35   Using computer conferencing for open learning
36   Using multimedia for open learning
37   Using the Internet for open learning

This chapter should not really be separate from other parts of this book! The parts on computer-conferencing, e-mail, multimedia and uses of the Internet are directly relevant to supporting open learners, and other parts of the chapter are relevant to the design of materials themselves. However, the thread which brings the elements of this chapter together is that all of the topics involve communications and information technologies in one way or another, and this field is seen by many as a dimension in its own right. My own view is that there is a significant danger in getting carried away with the medium at the expense of the message in some of the topic areas addressed here, and it is for this reason that I wanted to bring all of these elements into one arena for discussion, so that my central purpose could be offering suggestions to use each of these media as tools in an integrated toolkit, using each for what it is most appropriate for in the context of helping to make open learning successful.

I start by looking at one of the most common additions to print-based open learning packages: video. This medium is very powerful and can bring to open learning packages much that simply cannot be addressed by the printed word. However, we must remember that with television being a pervading influence in most people's lives, there is a tendency to *forget* most of that which we see on television screens. Therefore, using video for open learning needs to be particularly well planned if it is to be instrumental in helping students to learn. Next, I offer some suggestions about one of the cheapest, yet most neglected, media: audiotapes. Tone of voice, for example, can bring warmth and impact to words and ideas in ways which cannot be achieved through print.

The elements which make up the rest of this chapter are overlapping and interdependent. It is impossible to define where e-mail ends and computer-conferencing starts, other than by thinking of the respective intentions being one-to-one communication, and one-to-many or many-to-many communication. The Internet, if we are to regard it as a medium, allows and supports any of these means of communication, as well as providing a vast database of information, much of which is already interactive in its own right.

I suggest to readers of this chapter to treat the chapter as a whole rather than to become too preoccupied about the individual headings. In workshops that I lead, for example, on 'Using Technology to Enhance Learning', I find it productive to get people arguing about what, for example, is the difference between a computer-based learning package and a CD-ROM, as this helps them to think more deeply about what their learners actually *do* with each, in their own particular subject disciplines and topics. At the end of the day what matters most is that each and any of the media in this chapter is enhancing learning, rather than whether we have got the most appropriate classification or name for the technology itself.

# 31

# Using video for open learning

Video recordings are widely used in many forms of teaching and training, and already play valuable roles in helping to show open learners things that they would not be in a position to explore on their own. However, the act of watching material on a television screen is not one of the most powerful ways through which learners actually learn, unless the video extracts are carefully planned into their learning programme. The following suggestions may assist you to help your learners to make the most of video.

1   **Decide what the intended learning outcomes directly associated with the video extracts will be.** It is important that any video extracts are not just seen as an optional extra by your learners. The best way to prevent this from happening is to tell them exactly what they are intended to gain from each extract of video material.

2   **Decide why video is the best medium for your purposes.** Ask yourself 'what is this video extract doing that could not be done just in print?' Video extracts can be invaluable for showing all sorts of things that learners could not experience directly, as well as for conveying all of the subtleties that go with body language, facial expression, tone of voice, interpersonal interactions, skills and techniques.

3   **Decide *how* the video material is planned to help your learners to learn.** Is it primarily intended to whet their appetites and stimulate their motivation? Is it designed to help them to make sense of (or 'digest') some important ideas or concepts which are hard to learn without seeing things? Is it designed to give them useful briefings about things they themselves are intended to do after watching the material?

4   **Consider whether your learners will need their own copies of the material.** If they are intended to watch the video a number of times, and at their own choices of points during their studies, you may need to issue them with personal copies or make them available on loan. Alternatively, you may be able to arrange that the materials can be viewed on demand

in a learning resources centre. If so, make sure that there are mechanisms enabling learners to book a time-slot when they can see the video material, otherwise any difficulty in gaining access to the material could be cited as grounds for appeal against assessment decisions.

5   **Decide what your learners will take away after watching the video.** One of the dangers with video extracts is the 'now you see it, then it's gone' situation. If the video is serving important purposes for your learners, they will need to have something more permanent to remind them of what they learnt from it. Since, even if they have their own copies of the video material, they are unlikely to find time to revise from it directly, it is important that they have some other kind of summary of what they are expected to remember from it.

6   **Work out what (if anything) will be assessed.** If the video is just 'icing on the cake' and there is nothing arising from the video material that will be directly involved in any form of assessment, tell your learners that this is the case. When things they derive from using the video elements *are* involved in their assessment, explain this to them, to help them to give the video materials appropriate attention.

7   **Use short extracts at a time.** People are conditioned to watch quite long episodes of television, but to do so in a relatively passive way. Make sure that your learners approach video extracts in a different way than that which they normally use for watching television. It is better to split up a 30-minute video into half a dozen or so separate episodes if there are several different things you wish your learners to get out of the material. Some video materials have timings encoded onto the video tape.

8   **Set the agenda for your learners before each episode of video.** This can be done on the video extracts themselves, or in accompanying printed materials. Either way, ensure that your learners are set up with questions in their minds, to which the video extracts will provide answers.

9   **Consider giving your learners things to do while they view the video extracts.** You could brief them to note down particular observations, or to make particular decisions, or to extract and record specific facts or figures as they watch the video extracts.

10  **Consider asking your learners to do things after they have watched each extract.** This can help them to consolidate what they have gained from watching the extracts. It can also prompt them to have a further look at any extract where they may have slipped into passive viewing mode and missed important points.

11 **Don't underestimate the importance of printed support materials.** To make the most of video elements, learners need something in another medium to remind them about what they should be getting out of the video and where it fits into the overall picture of their learning. Video recordings often work best when supported by a printed workbook, into which learners write their observations and their interpretations of what they see. Their learning from such workbooks can be reviewed by looking again at them, even without looking again at the recording.

# 32

# Using audiotapes for open learning

Audiotape is so commonplace and cheap that its potential in open and flexible learning contexts is easily overlooked. In subject disciplines such as music, where sound is all important, the use of audiotapes as a learning medium is already well developed. In multimedia packages, sound and images are often combined to good effect, yet audiotape can sometimes play a similar role at much less cost. The use of audiotapes to support open learning can be extended to most disciplines. The following suggestions may help you to put audiotape to good use to support your learners.

1   **Have good reasons for using audiotapes.** Always be in a position to explain to your open learners *why* an audiotape is being used alongside their other learning resource materials. Share with them information on what they should be getting out of using the audiotape.

2   **Most learners have access to audiotape.** Many learners have portable cassette players, and may use these when travelling on public transport, or jogging, or driving and in all sorts of circumstances. When elements of open learning packages are available as audiotapes, there is the possibility that you will extend their learning to times when they would not otherwise be attempting to study.

3   **Label audiotapes informatively.** People who listen to tapes tend to accumulate lots of them, and it is easy for audiocassettes accompanying learning programmes to get lost amid those used for entertainment.

4    **Keep audiotape extracts short and sharp.** When there are specific intentions about what learners should get out of listening to audiotapes, extracts should normally last for a few minutes rather than quarters of an hour! It is worth starting each extract with a recorded 'name' such as 'Extract 3, to go with Section 1, Part 2', and to have the same voice reminding learners that when they have reached the 'End of extract 3, going with Section 1, Part 2', and so on.

5    **Use audiotape where tone of voice is important.** It can be particularly useful for open learners to hear messages, where the emphasis that you place on key words or phrases helps them to make sense of material which would be harder to interpret from a printed page or from a computer screen.

6    **Sound can help open learners into subject-related jargon.** When there is new terminology, for example, it can be hard to tell how to pronounce a word just by seeing it in print, and it can be humiliating for learners to find only when talking to a tutor that they have got their pronunciation wrong! Audiotapes can introduce the vocabulary of a subject to open learners.

7    **Use audiotapes to bring open learning to life.** Audiotapes can be invaluable for giving open learners the chance to hear people talking, discussing, debating, arguing, persuading, counselling, criticising, and can capture and pass on to them many experiences and processes which would be difficult to capture in print.

8    **Clarify exactly when a recorded episode should be used.** If you are using audiotape alongside printed materials, it can be useful to have a visual 'flag' to indicate to your learners when they should listen to a recorded extract.

9    **Turn open learners' listening into an active process.** Listening can all too easily be a passive process. Avoid this by setting your learners things to think about before listening to a tape extract. Prime them with a few questions, so that they will be searching for the answers from what they hear.

10   **When using audiotape to help your learners achieve particular outcomes, explain exactly what they should be getting out of listening to the tape.** It is useful to build in to your learning materials, activities which help your learners to reflect on, and make sense of, what they have been listening to on the tape.

11   **Consider using audiotape to give open learners feedback on their tutor-marked assignments.** If you are tutoring open learners, it can be quicker to talk for a few minutes into a tape recorder than to write all of your feedback down on your learners' written assignments. The added intimacy of tone of voice can help you to deliver critical feedback in a more acceptable form. Learners can also play the tape again and again, until they have understood each part of your recorded feedback. Always try to begin and end with something positive, just as you would do with written feedback.

12   **Combine audio and visual learning.** For example, it can be useful to use audiotape to talk open learners through things that they are looking at in their learning materials. For example, complex diagrams or derivations in printed materials, or graphics, tables, spreadsheets shown on-screen in computer-based materials can be brought to life by the sound of a human voice explaining what to look for in them.

# 33

# Using computer-based open learning packages

Computer-based packages are widely used in teaching and training and play a valuable part in open learning programmes. They have largely been developed for the open learning market. The following suggestions may help you to build appropriate computer-based packages wisely and effectively into your open learning contexts.

1   **Choose your packages carefully.** The best computer-based learning packages are not always those which look most attractive, nor are they necessarily the most expensive ones. The best indicator of a good package is evidence that they cause learning to be successful. Where possible, try them out on learners before committing yourself to purchasing them. Alternatively, ask the supplier or manufacturer for details of clients who have already used the packages, and check that the packages really deliver what you need.

2   **Get familiar with the package before letting your learners loose with it.** There is a learning curve to be ascended with most computer-based packages, and it is best if *you* go up this ahead of your open learners. They will need help on how to make best use of the package, as well as on what they are supposed to be learning from it.

3   **Check the intended learning outcomes of the computer-based package.** The main danger is that such packages address a wider range of intended outcomes than are needed by your open learners, and that learners may become distracted and end up learning things that they do not need to, possibly interfering with their assessment performance.

4  **If necessary, rephrase the learning outcomes associated with the package.** It may be useful to tell your open learners exactly what the learning outcomes mean in the context of their particular studies. This will help them to concentrate on the most important things in the package.

5  **Think about access to equipment and software.** It can be prohibitively expensive to give or loan each learner both the software and the hardware needed. However, if the package is an important part of their overall programme, ways need to be found to maximize their opportunity to work with it. Some packages come with licence arrangements to use the package with a given number of learners, either allowing multiple copies to be made or the package to be used over a network. Ensure that the software is protected to prevent unauthorized copying or unlicensed use on more than one machine.

6  **Think how learners will retain important ideas from the package after they have used it.** Make sure that there is supporting documentation or workbook materials, as these will help learners to summarize and remember the important things they gain while using computer-based packages. Where such resources do not already exist, you should consider the benefits of making a workbook or an interactive handout, so that learners working through the package write down things (or record them) at important stages in their learning.

7  **Ensure that learning-by-doing is appropriate and relevant.** Most computer-based packages contain a considerable amount of learning-by-doing, particularly decision-making, choosing options and entering responses to structured questions. Some of the tasks may not be entirely relevant to the intended learning outcomes of your open learning programme, and you may need to devise briefing details to help learners to see exactly what they should be taking seriously as they work through the package.

8  **Check that learners will get adequate feedback on their work with the package.** Much of this feedback may already be built in to the package as it stands. However, you may need to think about further ways of keeping track of whether your learners are getting what they should from their use of the package. It can be worth adding appropriate, short elements to tutor-marked assignments, so that there is a way of finding out whether particular learners are missing vital things they should have picked up from the package.

9   **Check how long the package should take.** The time spent by learners should be reflected in the learning payoff they derive from their studies with the package, and this in turn should relate to the proportion of the overall assessment framework that is linked to the topics covered by the package. Many computer-based learning packages come with indications of the expected timescales that are involved in using them, but it is well worth finding out how long typical learners actually take. Some computer-based packages can make this easier for you by logging the amount of time individuals spend working through them.

10  **Think ahead to assessment.** Work out what will be assessed, relating directly to the learning that is to be done using the computer-based materials. Express this as assessment criteria and check how these link to the intended learning outcomes. Make sure that learners, before working through the computer-based materials, know *what* will be assessed, *when* it will be assessed and *how* it will be assessed.

11  **Explore software that tracks learners.** Many computer-based materials can be used to track individual learners' progress through them. This can involve pre-testing and post-testing, storing the data on the computer system, as well as monitoring and recording the time taken by each learner to work through each part of the package. Such data can be invaluable for discovering the main problems that learners may be experiencing with the topic and with the package itself.

12  **Seek feedback from your learners.** Ask them what aspects of the package they found most valuable and most important. Ask them also what, if anything, went wrong in their own work with the package. Look at the feedback you obtain for anything that throws light on particular categories of learners finding difficulties with learning from the package (for example, speakers of other languages, or mature students, or people who are uncomfortable with new technologies). Where possible, find alternative ways of addressing important learning outcomes for those learners who have particular problems with the computer-delivered materials.

# 34

# Using e-mail to support open learning

Electronic communication is addictive! To most people who have already climbed the learning curve of finding out how to use e-mail, the apprehension they may have experienced on their first encounters fades into insignificance. E-mail can be an important medium in open learning. The following suggestions may help you to maximize some of the benefits it can offer to you and to your learners.

1  **Make sure that learners get started with e-mail.** Write careful, step-by-step briefing instructions for your learners. The computer literate people may hardly do more than glance at these before getting into the swing of using e-mail. However, for those people who lack confidence or experience with computers, these instructions can be vital and comforting until they become familiar with the medium.

2  **Decide what you really want to do with e-mail.** There are numerous purposes that e-mail can serve, and you need to ensure that the purpose is always clear to your learners. If they know *what* it is being used for, and *why* e-mail has been chosen for this, they are much more likely to get more out of it.

3  **Make the most of e-mail.** Although you may just want to use e-mail for routine communication with (and between) learners, there are many more uses that the medium can lend itself to. Think about the possible uses of sending attached files, such as documents, assignments, digitally-stored images, sounds and video recordings. All of these can be edited or marked, and returned to learners, in the same ways as simple messages.

4    **Make most messages really brief and to the point.** Few people take much notice of long e-mail messages. If something takes more than one screen, most readers either dump them or file them. Also encourage your learners to make good use of the medium, and to send several short messages rather than to try cramming lots of points into a single missive.

5    **Take particular care with your e-mail message titles.** It can take ages to search for a particular e-mail if it is not clear what each message is about. The computer software can sort messages by date and by sender, but it is more difficult to track down topics. Two or three well chosen keywords make the most useful titles.

6    **When you send a long e-mail, explain why and what to do with it.** For example, from time to time you may want to send learners something that you do not expect them to treat as a normal e-mail message, but perhaps to print out and study in depth. It makes all the difference if they know what they are expected to do with longer messages.

7    **Think about using e-mail to give feedback on assessed work.** It can be much quicker to compose e-mail replies to individual learners than to annotate their written work. It is also quite easy to give feedback on work submitted electronically, such as by adding *your* comments and notes in upper case to distinguish them from the original work, or (if your system permits this) by using a different colour or an alternative font for your feedback.

8    **Make the most of the lack of time constraints.** One of the most significant advantages of e-mail as a vehicle for feedback is that learners can view the feedback when they have time to make sense of it. They can store it until such time becomes available. They can also look at it as often as they wish to, and you can keep copies of exactly what you said to each individual learner.

9    **Be available!** When learners are accustomed to e-mail, they expect quick replies to their queries. If you are going to be away from your access to the system for more than a day or two at a time, it is worth letting all your learners know when you will be back online.

10   **Make the most of the speed.** Giving feedback by e-mail to learners at a distance obviously reduces delays. The sooner learners get feedback on their work, the more likely it is that their own thinking is still fresh in their minds, and the feedback is therefore better understood.

11   **Encourage learners to reply about your feedback.** This lets you know that it has been received but, more importantly, gives them the chance to let you know how they *feel* about the feedback you have given to them, or the mark or grade that you have awarded them.

12   **Use e-mail to keep a dispersed or distant group of learners together.** Sending out circular notes not only helps individuals to feel part of a community of learners, but also reminds them about important matters such as assessment deadlines, or problems that have arisen with course materials or updates to interesting materials that have been discovered on the Internet.

13   **Remember those learners whose access to e-mail is difficult or impossible.** One of the disadvantages of using e-mail as a means of communication on open learning programmes is, that if some learners have problems with access, they can become significantly disadvantaged. You may need to find ways of compensating through other means for those things they miss out on.

# 35

# Using computer conferencing for open learning

There are several parallel names for this, including computer-mediated communication (CMC), computer-supported cooperative learning and, more simply, online learning. Whatever we call them, computer conferences can be of great value in open learning schemes, especially where the learners are geographically dispersed, but working on similar timescales. Many of the suggestions made about e-mail continue to apply, but in this section I would like to alert you to some of the additional factors to consider with computer conferences. The following suggestions may help you to maximize the benefits that your learners can derive from computer conferencing.

1   **Note the differences between computer conferencing and other forms of electronic communication.** The distinguishing feature of computer conferencing is that many people can see the same contents from different places and at any time. The contents 'grow' as further notes and replies are added by participants. Most systems automatically alert participants to 'new messages' that have been added since they last viewed the conference, and allow these messages to be read first if desired.

2   **Regard computer conferences as virtual classrooms, seminar rooms and libraries.** Computer conferences can be each of these. They can provide a virtual classroom, where the whole student group can 'meet'. They can be used to provide a virtual seminar room, closed to all but a small learning group of around six students. They can function as virtual libraries, where resource banks and materials are kept. They can also function as student-only gossip areas. Each of these ways of using computer conferences can emulate electronically the related best practice in face-to-face learning environments.

3   **Get involved in computer conferencing situations yourself first.** If you have access to e-mail or the Internet, one of the best ways to pave the way towards putting computer conferencing to good use with your open learners is to participate yourself. For example, join some discussion lists and experience at first hand the things that work and the things that go wrong with such means of communication.

4   **Explore the computer conferencing systems from which you can choose.** There are several systems available around the world, each with their own formats, features and idiosyncrasies. If most of your open learners are not particularly computer literate, go for a system that makes it as easy as possible to log-on and to add messages.

5   **Make sure that all of your open learners will be able to access all the conferences which you want them to.** Ideally, you may also intend them to be able to download and/or print chosen extracts from the conference for their own personal study purposes. You can only build a computer conference into an open learning programme as an essential component if all of your learners are able to participate. If the conference is just an optional extra for those able to join it, other learners who cannot may be able to claim to have been disadvantaged.

6   **Provide good 'start-up' pages.** These are essentially the main topics of the conference and are listed sequentially in the main directory of the conference. Conferencing takes place when participants add 'replies' to these pages. The replies are normally listed in the sub-directory of each start-up page in the order in which they are received.

7   **Make each screen speak for itself.** Especially with 'start-up' pages, which introduce each topic in the conference, it is best that the essence of the main message takes up less than a single screen. Further detail can be added in the next few pages (or 'replies'). Encourage learners contributing their own replies to keep them to a single screen whenever possible, and to send several replies with different titles rather than one long reply addressing a number of different aspects.

8   **Use the conference as a notice board.** Get into the habit of making the conference *the* best way to keep up with topical developments in the field of study, as well as administrative matters such as assessment deadlines, guidance for learners preparing assessments, and so on. Try to make it necessary for learners to log-on to the conference regularly; this will result in a greater extent of active contribution by them.

9    **Use the conference as a support mechanism.** This can save a lot of tutor time. Elements of explanation, advice or counselling that otherwise may have had to be sent individually to several different open learners can be put into the conference once only and remain available to all. Whenever your reply to an enquiry or problem raised by an open learner warrants a wider audience, the conference is there to do this.

10   **Make the conference a resource in its own right.** Add some screens of useful resource material, maybe with 'hot-links' to other Internet sources that are relevant. It is useful if some such material is *only* available through the computer conference; this ensures that all your learners will make efforts to use it.

11   **Try to get learners discussing and arguing with each other via the conference.** The best computer conferences are not just tutor–student debates, but are taken over by the students themselves. They can add new topics, and bring a social dimension to the conference.

12   **Consider having some assessed work entered onto the conference.** If learners *have* to make some contributions, they are more likely to ascend the learning curve regarding sending in replies, and to do so more readily in non-assessed elements too. One advantage in having an assessed task 'up on the conference' is that each open learner can see everyone else's attempts, and the standards of work improve very rapidly.

13   **Think about the possibilities afforded by audio-conferencing and video-conferencing.** Either, or both, of these processes can be used very effectively to support open learners to help them to learn from each other and to reduce their isolation. Some of my suggestions about audiotapes and video, mentioned earlier in this chapter, can be linked with the advice above about interaction and communication, to make audio-conferencing and video-conferencing play valuable roles. In particular, it is important to ensure that there are definite, agreed purposes for each occasion where such conferences are used, as well as the freedom to follow up matters which arise during each conference.

# 36

# Using multimedia for open learning

Learning packages can contain, or refer out to, an increasing range of other kinds of material. We explored the use of videotapes in a separate set of suggestions, but the present set aims to alert you to the questions you should be asking yourself about *any* medium. This could range from CD-ROMs, the Internet, intranets, interactive videos, and anything which adds sounds, still pictures, moving images, graphics to the experience of learners working through open learning materials.

1  **How does the medium help open learners' motivation?** Ideally, any multimedia component should help open learners to want to learn from them. If there are too many steps to getting going with the multimedia elements, there is the danger that learners can be put off and maybe stopped in their tracks.

2  **Can the medium be used to provide some learning-by-doing?** Perhaps the biggest danger with some multimedia packages is that however sophisticated the media used, open learners may only be spectators rather than players. Where it is not possible to cause learners to interact directly with the materials, it remains possible to get them to make decisions, answer questions, summarize conclusions and to write down these for later reference.

3  **Can the medium be used to give open learners feedback?** The danger is that the information presented using multimedia is often fixed, and cannot then respond to what open learners may be thinking about it, or to the problems or misunderstandings that may be in their minds. It is best to ensure that some self-assessment questions address directly any important information presented in multimedia formats, so that feedback responses can be designed for learners to address such difficulties.

4   **How does the medium help open learners to make sense of things?** There are often excellent answers to this question. For example, sounds, pictures, moving images and colourful graphics can all play useful parts in helping open learners to get their heads around things with which they have been grappling.

5   **Why is this medium better than other, cheaper media?** For example, why is a computer-based package better than a print-based one? There are many good answers to this question. The best answers are when the medium chosen does something that just cannot be done by other media, for example, moving pictures showing body language and facial expression, where such dimensions are crucially important for getting particular messages or attitudes across to open learners.

6   **How relevant will the medium-based element be to the overall learning programme?** One of the dangers with media-based learning is that too much 'nice-to-know' material may be involved, and not enough emphasis placed on 'need-to-know' material, and that open learners may not easily be able to distinguish the two categories.

7   **How will the choice of medium affect open learners' opportunities to learn?** For example, will they only be able to study the particular elements concerned when they are sitting at a networked computer terminal or when logged on to the Internet? Will this mean that they have frequently to stop learning until they can gain such access? Will there be alternative coverage of these elements of learning for any learners who have not got easy access to the medium, and can it be guaranteed that they will not end up disadvantaged?

8   **How easy will it be to edit and change the medium-based elements?** Open learning materials are never 'finished'. There are always adjustments and changes that are indicated from piloting, feedback from learners and from assessments measuring how well learners actually succeeded in their learning. Some media are much easier to edit and change than others. Changing a CD-ROM or videodisk is a much more complex (and more expensive) business than changing a file in a computer-based package.

9   **What *other* media could have been used?** There is rarely just one way to package up a particular element of learning. It is useful to explore at least two or three alternative ways of using media to deliver each element of learning, and then to make an informed decision about *why* a particular medium is chosen.

10  **How will learners revise and consolidate what they have learnt from the medium?** What will they have to take away? Will they be able to make a structured summary of what they learnt while working with the medium, which will bring all the important points back to their minds when looking at it later?

# 37

# Using the Internet for open learning

In a way, the Internet *is* open learning. People can use it at times of their own choice, in their own ways, at their own pace and from anywhere that access to it is available to them. That said, this does not mean that it is automatically a vehicle for productive and effective learning. Indeed, it is very easy to become side-tracked by all sorts of fascinating things, and to stray well away from any intended learning outcome. The suggestions which follow are not intended as starting points for setting out to *deliver* open learning through the Internet (this is indeed possible, but could take a whole book to explore properly), but rather to help open learners to *use* the Internet to obtain material to use in connection with their studies, such as in assignments they are preparing. The following suggestions may help you to help your open learners both to enjoy the Internet *and* to learn well from it.

1 **Play with the Internet yourself.** You need to pick up your own experience of how it feels to tap into such a vast and varied database, before you can design ways of delivering it to your open learners with some meaningful learning experiences.

2 **Decide whether you want your open learners to use the Internet or an Intranet.** An Intranet is where a networked set of computers talk to each other while using Internet conventions, but where the content is not open to the rest of the universe. If you are working in an organization which already has such a network, and if your open learners can make use of this network effectively, there will be some purposes that will be better served by the Intranet. You can also have *controlled* access to the Internet via an Intranet, such as by using hot-links to predetermined external sites.

3   **Use the Internet to research something yourself.** You may well, of course, have already done this often, but if not, give it a try before you think of setting your open learners 'search and retrieve' tasks with the Internet. Set yourself a fixed time, perhaps half an hour or even less. Choose a topic that you are going to search for, preferably something a little offbeat. See for yourself how best to use the search engines and compare the efficiency of different engines. Find out for yourself how to deal with 4,593 references to your chosen topic, and how to improve your searching strategy to whittle them down to the ten that you really want to use!

4   **Don't just use the Internet as a filing cabinet for your teaching resources!** While it is useful in its own way if your open learners can have access to your own notes and teaching–learning resources, this is not really *using* the Internet. Too many materials designed for use in other forms are already cluttering up the Internet. If all you intend your open learners to do is to download your notes and print their own copies, sending them e-mailed attachments would do the same job much more efficiently.

5   **Think carefully about your intended learning outcomes.** You may indeed wish to use the Internet as a means whereby your open learners address the existing intended outcomes associated with their subject material. However, it is also worth considering whether you may wish to add further learning outcomes to do with the processes of searching, selecting, retrieving and analysing subject material. If so, you may also need to think about whether, and how, these additional learning outcomes may be assessed.

6   **Give your open learners specific things to do using the Internet.** Make these tasks, where it is relevant, involve up-to-the-minute data or news, rather than where the 'answers' are already encapsulated in easily accessible books or learning resources.

7   **Consider giving your open learners a menu of tasks and activities.** They will feel more ownership if they have a significant degree of choice in their Internet tasks. Where you have a group of open learners working on the same syllabus, it can be worth letting them choose different tasks, and then communicating their main findings to each other (and to you) using a computer conference or by e-mail.

8   **Let your open learners know that the process is at least as important as the outcome.** The key skills that they can develop using the Internet include designing an effective search and making decisions about the quality and authenticity of the evidence they find. It is worth designing tasks where you already know of at least some of the evidence you expect them to locate, and remaining open to the fact that they will each uncover at least as much again as you already know about!

9    **Consider designing your own interactive pages.** You may want to restrict these to an Intranet, at least at first. You can then use dialogue boxes to cause your open learners to answer questions, enter data, and so on. Putting such pages up for all to see on the Internet may mean that you get a lot of unsolicited replies!

10   **Consider getting your open learners to design and enter some pages.** This may be best done restricted to an Intranet, at least until your learners have picked up sufficient skills to develop pages that are worth putting up for all to see. The act of designing their own Internet material is one of the most productive ways to help your open learners to develop their critical skills at evaluating materials already on the Internet.

# Chapter 5  Supporting open learners

38    Tutoring open learners
39    Training open learning tutors
40    Giving tutor feedback to open learners
41    Helping open learners to develop learning skills
42    Helping open learners to help each other
43    Mentoring open learners

While it is possible to package up information and knowledge in a wide variety of media, and to design into open and flexible learning all of the processes whereby learning should be successful, human beings remain an indispensable agency for guaranteeing the success of open and flexible learning. Human beings can do more to warm up learners' enthusiasm, interest and their thirst for learning than any other medium. Human beings can also all too readily destroy any of these! It is, therefore, crucial that tutors supporting open learners do so in ways that maximize learners' motivation and success.

I start this chapter by offering some suggestions about some of the differences between tutoring open learners and supporting students working through conventional face-to-face programmes. To support open learners well, appropriate tutor training opportunities need to be made available to tutors. In practice, most teachers or lecturers, who are good at supporting conventional students can rapidly extend their skills to supporting students using other modes of studying. However, facing up to the differences can make a radical difference to how well open learning tutoring is achieved.

The most critical side of supporting open learners is giving feedback on their marked work. I offer some suggestions to help you to make sure that the time and energy you invest in giving feedback to open learners is well spent. Part of the support that tutors can give open learners is about *how* best they should approach their learning. Simply reading about study skills approaches to open learning has very limited value. Printed advice tends to be read and acted on by those learners who actually least need it! I follow my suggestions on study skills strategies with a discussion of ways that tutors can help open learners to make the most of each and every opportunity of working collaboratively with each other. For students studying one or two flexible learning elements alongside other college-based modules, there is ample opportunity for them to find times and places where they can talk to each other about their progress with their open learning. In particular, encouraging students to explain difficult areas to each other is beneficial. Where students do not have such opportunities to meet face-to-face, communications media such as e-mail and computer conferencing can be an effective substitute.

I end this chapter with some suggestions on setting up mentoring for open learners. It can be particularly valuable to have mentoring as well as tutoring. Another human being, *not* wearing an assessment hat, can be a powerful source of motivation for open learners, and can troubleshoot many of their potential problems with them.

# 38

# Tutoring open learners

Most open learning schemes use some kind of tutor support. Often, tutors are responsible not only for encouraging learners and helping to keep them going, but also for marking (and sometimes setting) assignments. Tutor support may be done entirely from a distance, or face to face with small groups of open learners, or indeed face to face with individual open learners, depending on the way the open learning system is structured. In any of these modes, good tutor support can make a great deal of difference to open learners' motivation and completion rates. The following suggestions should help you to be an effective supporter of open learners.

1   **Remember that you're a very important person.** For some of your open learners, your support and help will make all the difference between them passing or failing (or dropping out). You may be the only human contact in the context of the particular learning that you are supporting. Even a few minutes of your time, whether over the phone, through the post, or by e-mail, may be vital to them during times of difficulty.

2   **Don't expect all of your learners to need you equally.** While it is wise to try to treat all learners equally, some will make relatively little demand on your time, while others will need more help. Most open learning tutors find that on any programme there are one or two learners who take almost as much time as most of the others put together!

3   **Try to get to know your learners.** This is obviously easier if you have the chance to meet them from time to time, for example at face-to-face tutorials. However, even if you do not meet them, it is surprising how quickly you can get to know at least some of them. Even when communication is restricted to written comments or e-mail communication, some learners are easy to get to know.

4   **Find out what to call your open learners.** You will normally have records about them, including such basics as name, address, perhaps age, maybe employment details, and so on. However, such information may not tell you whether William prefers to be written to as Bill, especially if he signs his letters and forms as W R Roversworth, or whether he may actually be Reg! Getting people's names right is so important. If they feel you do not even know who they are, they will not put much trust in your support.

5   **Let them know a bit about you.** Especially in open learning systems where students do not meet their tutors, it can make a big difference to establishing an effective working relationship with them when learners know a bit about their tutors' backgrounds, and even their main fields of interest. Take care, however, not to say so much about your experience and qualifications that learners feel intimidated. A few words about your main leisure interests can work surprisingly well in opening up communication to at least some of your learners.

6   **Your written words are very important to open learners.** Don't write without due consideration as to how learners may *feel* when they read your comments on their work. Some learners will read your comments over and over again, and may seek depths of meaning that you did not anticipate when you wrote them. Remember that it is not possible to undo something that you have put in writing.

7   **Keep channels of communication reasonably open.** Make it clear to all of your open learners if you are going to be away from your phone or your desk for days on end. When learners have a problem or enquiry, they can get quite upset if there is no response for what seems to them like a long time. If they know in advance that there will be certain times when you are not there, they are much better at waiting.

8   **Let learners know how, where and when to contact you.** If your tutoring system involves telephone support, remember that some learners will be quite shy in disturbing such an important person as you, whether at home or at work. Let them know good times when to ring you up and where. If they ring at inconvenient times, and realize that this is so, they can become even more nervous about contacting you by phone. It is better to have some definite, even if quite limited, times when they can expect you to be ready and waiting to hear from them.

9   **Provide *extra* help or information sometimes.** For example, when your learners are about to start that difficult 'Section 5' of their materials, it can help them a lot if you send out your own sheet (or e-mail) of personal advice about how best to go about studying the section.

10  **Make the most of face-to-face opportunities.** When open or flexible learning elements are integrated into college-based programmes, tutors or lecturers often see their open learning students in other contexts, including large-group lectures or smaller-group seminars or tutorials. It is important that any of these face-to-face contexts are fine tuned to accommodate the open learning which may be going on in parallel to them. Face-to-face contact can achieve a great deal in supporting open learning, and can be a springboard for encouraging students to work collaboratively as well as independently at their open learning studies.

11  **Keep good records.** If one of your learners phones you unexpectedly, or writes with an urgent question or message, it is important that you are seen to know exactly everything that you could have known about this learner's progress so far, and any other relevant data about the learner's particular situation or circumstances.

# 39

# Training open learning tutors

Most people who become open learning tutors have some experience of teaching in other contexts. However, supporting learners at a distance, or even learners working independently in a college or training resources centre, involves new and different skills. There is considerable transferability of skills, however, and effective face-to-face tutors usually manage the transition splendidly. The following suggestions may alert you to the sorts of training which can help open learning tutors to develop quickly the necessary skills and competences.

1  **Help tutors to introduce themselves to open learners.** For example, ask each tutor in a group to prepare an overhead transparency of some 'about your tutor' information and show the overheads to the group. Ask each member of the group to role-play learners, and to 'Pick the tutor you would feel best about' from these introductions. Then look in more detail at what it is in the most successful introductions that causes them to work well.

2  **Remind tutors that in written feedback much human warmth can be lost.** For example, learners cannot see the smile or the twinkle in their tutor's eye. There is no tone of voice to soften critical feedback. Also, written feedback cannot be retrieved and reworded. It is important to get it right first time. Open learners whose relationship with their tutors has been damaged by careless or inappropriate written feedback may never entirely recover from the experience.

3  **Build in some practice at giving written feedback.** The wording and tone of feedback to open learners from tutors is so important, that it cannot just be left to chance. Tutors need feedback on how their words will be received by typical open learners, and especially by those who are more sensitive than most. Get tutors to write extracts of their comments to learners on overhead transparencies, and get the group of tutors to look for words or phrases which could demotivate or upset sensitive learners. Such phrases include, 'you have failed to grasp the basics of...', but even the word 'however' is often followed by bad news.

4    **Help tutors to become better at giving positive feedback.** The danger is that when learners get things right, tutors just tick them, or restrict their feedback to a good score or grade. Open learners need encouragement and praise even more than face-to-face students do. We all do, of course! Even short written comments on their work can help, such as 'yes indeed', 'absolutely', 'very good point', or 'I totally agree'.

5    **Help tutors to become better at giving critical feedback.** This is close to the art of effective tutoring of open learners! For example, learners working alone at a distance may need the sort of reassurance about things they get wrong by using phrases such as, 'Most people have trouble with this concept at first' or, 'Don't worry, this will get easier'.

6    **Give tutors some practice at telephone communication.** It is not necessary to use telephones for this practice; what is important is that there are both an observer and a recipient. The most useful way of providing this practice is to set up exercises where tutors explain something to someone else by role-playing an open learner, with a third person looking for things that aid communication and things that get in the way.

7    **Build in some practice at assessing.** In most open learning schemes, an important part of the work of tutors is assessing learners' work on tutor-marked assignments. While the tone and nature of feedback is important, it is also vital to make sure that the assessment is valid and reliable, especially when the same assignments are being marked by a number of tutors in parallel. Give a group of tutors two or three past assignments to 'mark' privately, then collect and discuss all of the scores or grades.

8    **Help tutors to be able to deal with learners' problems.** This is best done using case-study exercises, and getting tutors to write, e-mail or use the telephone in response to a range of students' problems or crises. Tutors learn a great deal very quickly from seeing how each other might handle such scenarios.

9    **Alert tutors to ways they can gather feedback on their tutoring from open learners.** Explore the potential of questions such as, 'what was the most useful thing you found about my comments on your last assignment?' and, 'what would you particularly like me to tell you about in connection with the work you are sending in next?'

10    **Encourage tutors to be open learners themselves.** There is nothing better than being in the same position as your open learners for helping tutors to be sensitive, effective and fair.

# 40

# Giving tutor feedback to open learners

There is no single factor more crucial than the feedback that open learners receive on their progress. Some of this feedback is built in to their open learning materials, for example, in responses to self-assessment questions. Such feedback can only address identified agendas, or respond to anticipated difficulties or mistakes. Tutor feedback should add to this, particularly when dealing with concepts and issues where human judgement and human response is needed. In this section, I offer some more detailed suggestions about how to make tutor feedback play an optimum role in helping open learners to succeed.

1   **Think about learners' feelings.** The act of submitting some work for authoritative comment is quite daunting to many open learners. It may be an unusual situation for them to have the possibility of their work being criticized. For some open learners, it may be a long time since they had their work assessed. Learners often report feeling 'exposed', 'vulnerable', 'apprehensive' and even 'scared stiff' at the prospect of finding out how they have fared in tutor-marked assignments.

2   **Remember that learners are excited too.** As well as the feelings mentioned above, there are other strong emotions involved at the time of submitting an assignment for assessment. These include, 'I was glad to have pulled it all together and sent it in', 'I can't wait to see if I got it right', 'I don't want to do anything more until I find out how I did in this part'.

3   **Take particular care with written words.** Open learners can too easily take feedback about their work as though it is feedback about them as people! Make sure that any critical feedback is clearly about something that they have done, and not about them. Even such distinctions as those between 'Your answer to Question 3 missed out consideration of the causes involved' and 'You missed the causes of such-and-such' are significant.

4    **Keep your sentences short.** Don't use long words in your feedback comments when shorter ones would do. Your feedback messages need to get across to your learners without them having to try to analyse your writing to discover your meaning.

5    **Feedback should be as quick as possible.** When learners have tackled an assignment, feedback from tutors is much more effective if it is received while learners' thoughts on the work are still fresh in their minds. Ideally, it would be best for them to receive feedback within hours of submitting their work for assessment. This is, of course, not possible when the feedback is delivered by post to learners at a distance, but every day counts.

6    **Consider ways of giving quicker first draft feedback.** Tutors can sometimes send e-mail messages to learners, giving them the most important news about their work as soon as it is marked. Feedback can alternatively be sent by fax, which is more convenient for some open learners than e-mail, as faxes can reach them at work without them having to go somewhere to log-on to check for e-mail messages. The advantages of rapid feedback need to be balanced against the possibility that such quick feedback may not be as objective as more considered feedback. For example, tutors may only have a real perspective on the feedback they will give after marking *all* of a batch of assignments, when they can also give feedback on how each learner compares with the average performance in the group.

7    **Consider using the phone for some feedback.** This has the advantage that learners can ask questions, and tutors can make sure that learners understand the trickier issues that may be involved in the feedback. Also, tone of voice can do much to help learners to receive feedback which may have been more disappointing for them in writing, and tutors can sense how far to press critical comments from the tone of learners' responses over the phone.

8    **Don't make assumptions.** Even such a statement as 'you've obviously put a lot of work into this assignment' can be dangerous. There is no problem when the assumption turns out to be true, but if the work was actually rushed off at the last minute, such feedback immediately loses the tutor any credibility with the learner involved.

9    **Keep records of your feedback.** This is easier with those parts of your feedback where you have your own copy (for example, the multi-part pro formas that some open learning systems use to keep records of important summary feedback). It saves a lot of time to be organized about your record keeping. It is important to remember which learner is which when answering phone calls, or how many assignments the person you are talking to has already done.

10   **Make the most of the benefits that can be achieved through whole-group feedback opportunities.** For example, in college-based flexible learning systems, lecturers can use scheduled large-group sessions to give students whole-group feedback on their performance in tutor-marked assignments, perhaps by issuing and discussing with the group a handout applying to students' work in general on a particular assignment or question. This can be helpful in reducing the time that it takes to mark open learners' work, and delivering some of the most important feedback verbally to the whole group, rather than writing the same things repetitively on many students' assignments. It is particularly valuable for the students themselves to be able to gauge how their individual performance measures up to that of their fellow students, and to find out whether their individual difficulties with an assignment are in fact commonly shared problems.

11   **Seek feedback on your feedback.** Some open learners do indeed want their tutors to call a spade a spade. For others, it is better to tread much more carefully. Ask your learners for their reactions to your feedback. Ask them what they found most useful. Ask them which parts they found difficult or demotivating. Ask them how they felt about it. Try to tune your feedback to everything you know about each individual learner.

# 41

# Helping open learners to develop learning skills

One of the most significant benefits of open learning is that it helps people to become better at learning under their own steam. This is often more important than the subject-specific content of the programme, and is something that will help students for years after their open learning programme finishes. While the very process of open learning delivers such benefits quite naturally, human help can play a vital part. The following suggestions illustrate the role that can be played by open learning tutors in helping students to become better learners.

1   **Being an effective open learner does not just come naturally.** Although there is nothing fundamentally different about learning from open learning resources, the circumstances surrounding open learners are quite different from the situation at colleges or training courses. Therefore, it is an important part of the role both of open learning tutors and writers to help students to become better at taking charge of their own learning.

2   **Reinforce the benefits of open learning.** Remind your open learners of the advantages of being in charge of their own learning, and choosing the times and places to learn that suit them best. Help them see the benefits of learning at their own pace, and being able to go back to anything at any time to make sure that they have still got a grip on it. Point out that self-assessment questions and feedback responses give them the luxury of privacy in which to make mistakes!

3   **Don't underplay the limitations of open learning.** Remind learners working on their own that they may be missing out on peer-group support. Help them to find ways of compensating for this, such as opening up channels of communication (postal or electronic) with other students learning the same things.

4   **When possible, choose open learning materials that help students to learn.** The materials that work best for open learning are those where the *process* of how best to learn is addressed in tandem with the topic that is unfolding. Some materials have study skills tips in boxes throughout them, or help menus on-screen that can be explored by learners finding something difficult.

5   **Help learners to confront their motivation.** Help them to explore *why* they are learning. Help them to see what is in it for them. Help them to see the benefits that can come to them when they have learnt successfully. An important part of an open learning tutor's role is to help learners to *want* to learn.

6   **Help learners to see why they may *need* to learn things.** This is important for the more difficult or less interesting parts of a topic, where it may be quite hard to find any real reasons for *wanting* to learn them. If you can provide good answers to the question, 'Why do I need to do all this?', you can help your learners to find that extra bit of persistence that they may need to get to grips with something that you know they will need.

7   **Help learners to make the most of learning-by-doing.** Most open learning materials (or at least most effective ones) are full of opportunities for learning-by-doing. These include self-assessment questions, exercises, practical activities, and so on. Tutor-marked assignments also involve learning-by-doing, but those learners who skip everything else are missing out on many of their chances to learn. Help learners to see that all this extra practice is not to be squandered, and that self-assessment exercises pave the way to success in the assignments that follow.

8   **Discuss with learners the different approaches that they need for different modes of study.** Where students are undertaking only one or two areas by open or flexible learning, and spending the rest of their time in college-based, traditional teaching–learning situations, there is a strong tendency for them not to enter fully into good study approaches for their open learning. For example, they often tend to skip the self-assessment questions, and merely concentrate on preparing for the questions that happen to be visible in the tutor-marked assignments. This means that they miss out the valuable learning-by-doing associated with the whole module, and only enter into selected parts of it.

9    **Remind open learners of the benefits of getting things wrong in the comfort of privacy.** Well-designed self-assessment questions allow students to learn from their mistakes. It is worth emphasising how useful this can be to open learners. Learning from mistakes can be much more memorable than simply getting things right first time, especially where there is no embarrassment or loss of face in making errors. Keep reminding open learners that self-assessment questions are just as valuable to them when they get them wrong as when they get them right, and that the only way to lose out on them is to skip them.

10   **Prepare learners to make the most of feedback.** Where there are well-designed feedback responses built into the learning materials, make sure that your open learners know how much value they can derive from these. Help them to see the value of working out *why* they made any mistakes. Suggest to them that they repeat the self-assessment exercises from time to time, so that they make better sense of the feedback and remind themselves of what they got right or where they went wrong in the past.

11   **Build study skills guidance into your own feedback.** When you encounter learners who are struggling with a concept or a task, work out how to advise them to adjust their approach. Think back to how you yourself originally made sense of the topic concerned. Talk to other people who have succeeded with it, and ask them for tips for someone for whom the light has not yet dawned on the topic.

12   **Help learners to find out about the assessment culture.** Help them to see what scores marks and what loses marks. For example, make sure that each tutor-marked assignment comes with full details of the marking scheme that will be used. Consider setting an additional self-assessed assignment, where learners themselves apply a marking scheme to something they have done, and then get feedback from you on whether their assessment has been objective.

13   **Help your learners to prepare for any formal assessments.** When open learning programmes lead into traditional unseen written exams, for example, learners often feel very nervous about this prospect. While there is a wealth of material on revision and exam strategies that learners can *read*, it makes a great deal of difference to them to have someone that they can talk to about it, or write to explaining their worries.

# 42

# Helping open learners to help each other

Open learners working on their own at a distance can be quite lonely. Even college students do not always take full advantage of the fact that they are often surrounded by people experiencing the same problems and difficulties. The following suggestions point towards ways of helping learners to make the most of each other, whether at a distance or working together.

1   **Help open learners to appreciate the benefits they can derive from other learners.** Where students are separated by distance, there is the danger that they can feel quite isolated from other people learning at the same time. The most significant step is helping learners to *want* contact with other learners. That leads them to make the most of any opportunities you can provide for peer-group support and feedback.

2   **Help open learners to get to know each other.** Most open learners, even working separately at a distance, are willing to make contact with other people in the same position. To do this, it is useful if they have not only contact names, addresses, phone numbers and e-mail details, but also short 'bionotes' on each other. Once the hurdle of opening up contact is overcome, open learners are usually more than willing to maintain contact, and the exchanges between them contribute significantly to their learning and their motivation.

3   **Make the most of any face-to-face opportunities.** College-based flexible learning pathways normally involve meetings, where all the students studying a module can get together with one or more tutors, to sort out problems and clarify any subject areas which may be causing difficulty. Such occasions provide students with a good opportunity to compare notes, and to gain a perspective on how they are getting on individually. Some distance learning programmes (notably those of the Open University in the UK) provide tutorials which serve similar purposes. However, the

greatest benefits can sometimes be associated with the networking that occurs between students before and after such meetings. Students soon see the value of this, and often arrange to meet from time to time without the presence of a tutor. Parallel benefits can be achieved through computer conferencing.

4   **Don't assume that students who already know each other will automatically help each other.** The loneliness of the distance learner may not seem to be a problem in circumstances where college-based students are working through selected parts of the curriculum in open learning mode. However, such students may feel because the open learning is designed to be done on an individual basis that they are expected to do it alone and not discuss it with other students. Legitimize and encourage collaboration.

5   **Explore the possibility of setting open learners collaborative tasks.** If it is feasible to make such collaboration part of an assessed task, so much the better, but then it is vital to ensure that all learners have appropriate opportunities for collaboration. While it is relatively easy to introduce collaborative tasks into flexible learning elements studied in college environments, it remains possible to do something similar with distance learners, particularly if they already have such means of communication as e-mail or computer conferencing.

6   **Help learners to realize that they are in an ideal position to 'teach' others.** Someone who has just mastered something is often the best person to explain it to others who are struggling. People who mastered it years ago may not remember how the light dawned.

7   **Show learners the value to them of teaching other people.** The act of explaining something to someone else is one of the best ways of 'getting one's head around it'. Explaining something a few times to different people leads to deeper understanding in the mind of the explainer. Furthermore, hearing a few different people explaining something helps learners to find their own ways of getting to grips with difficult ideas or concepts. The opportunity for open learners to have such explanations offered by tutors is usually quite limited, but the situation can be much improved by making full use of peer explanations.

8   **Explore the possibility of learners who have already succeeded helping newer learners.** In college-based programmes, the value of such coaching or 'proctoring' is well known. It can work too with open learning programmes. Some students who have already passed a module or study unit may be willing to help a few learners presently studying it. Care needs to be taken, however, that such coaching does not fall into sharing past assignments!

9    **Consider whether informal peer-assessment can help.** Getting open learners to apply assessment criteria to each others' work can pay significant dividends. Firstly, it is a way of letting learners see other people's answers to tasks and questions, each with strengths and weaknesses that are useful for them to judge. Secondly, it can lead to a deeper kind of communication between learners. Thirdly, peer-assessment is one of the most effective ways of letting learners in to the assessment culture, helping them to structure their learning and energy towards practices which will succeed in more formal assessment later.

10   **Don't, however, try to force learners into collaboration.** Some people choose distance learning for various reasons, including that they actually *want* to work on their own, in their own ways, and without pressure to communicate with others. Such motivation is usually high enough to compensate for what is lost by lack of communication. The penalty for manipulating such learners into unwanted communication can be that they decide that open learning is not, after all, really for them.

# 43

# Mentoring open learners

While in many open learning schemes, all the support that learners may need comes from their tutors, it is increasingly common to separate the support role from the assessment side of open learning. This is best done when there is someone else to do the general encouraging and coaxing. Mentor support can make a big difference to open learners' success rates, and can reduce non-completion significantly. The following suggestions may help you to see the potential of mentor support for your open learners.

1   **Work out what you really mean by 'a mentor'.** Most definitions of a mentor involve either or both the phrases 'trusted colleague' and 'critical friend'. It is desirable (but not essential) that a mentor should not have a conflict of interests, such as could be caused by having a managerial or supervisory role with the learners concerned, or being involved in some way in the learners' assessment or accreditation.

2   **If mentors have managerial roles too, help them to become able to 'switch hats'.** Some managers are able to perform quite different roles, and it is perfectly possible for a manager to mentor open learners, by keeping the supervisory and support roles quite distinct. For example, it can help if the place chosen for mentor–learner meetings is neutral territory, rather than the manager's office.

3   **Consider whether mentors need to know the subjects being studied.** Sometimes, open learners will have subject-specific questions or problems. Normally, it might be expected that such problems will be handled by a tutor rather than a mentor. However, tutorial support may be more difficult to get, and it may be easier for learners to ask mentors. In such cases, it is useful if the mentors themselves have time and opportunity to work through the open learning materials, so that they are well primed to deal with specific problems.

4   **Consider whether mentors are just there to keep learners going.** When mentors are not expected to deal with subject-specific matters, their most important role is then supporting learners and helping to make sure that they have no general obstacles in their way. The role of such mentors then becomes more general, and may need to be spelled out for the particular context in which learners are studying, so that both mentors and learners know how to handle the mentor–learner relationship.

5   **Establish guidelines for good practice for mentors.** Look at the kinds of help and support that mentors can provide to your open learners, in both the context of the level of their studies and the subject disciplines involved. It is useful to brainstorm with a group of mentors (and preferably also some experienced open learners), completions to the phrase, 'A good mentor will…' This can form the basis of a mentors' handbook, and also help open learners to understand what they can expect from their mentors.

6   **Run mentor training sessions.** Like open learning tutors, mentors need practice in handling their role. It can be useful to get a group of mentors together and explore the nature of the mentoring role with them. Get them to role-play to solve various 'mentoring dilemmas' based on typical problems that actual open learners have had, or may be anticipated to have.

7   **Build in particular things for mentors to do.** It is useful it there are a few 'necessary encounters' between open learners and their mentors at particular stages in the learners' studies. For example, a mentor debriefing after learners have got the results of their first important tutor-marked assignment can help learners to see that mentors are there to help them.

8   **Have ways of keeping track of mentors.** It is useful if there is some form of paperwork that shows meetings between mentors and learners and, particularly, decisions reached and actions taken on both sides. A brief record of meetings and their outcomes, preferably signed by both parties and kept by both, provides a way of helping to monitor that mentoring is indeed happening, and also helps to identify open learners whose progress may be slipping and who may need some additional support from mentors.

9   **Help mentors to learn from each other.** It is useful to have regular meetings between everyone in an organization who is involved in mentoring. This can lead to the exchange of ideas on, 'What I did when my open learner had difficulty with such-and-such'. If there is a healthy network of mentors, it is also easier for back-up cover for learners to be arranged when a mentor is going to be unavailable for a while.

10 **Allow time for mentoring.** Mentoring is an important role, and should not be squeezed into already full schedules, or done entirely on a good-will basis. Giving mentors some time allowance, or some additional payment, for the duties involved helps them to take the role seriously.

# Chapter 6 Assessing open learning

44 Designing tutor-marked assignments
45 Designing marking schemes for tutor-marked assignments
46 Monitoring the quality of tutor assessment
47 Designing computer-marked assignments
48 Designing computer-generated feedback to open learners
49 Designing multiple-choice exams
50 Diversifying the assessment of open learners
51 Piloting and adjusting open learning materials

Assessment can be described as the engine which drives learning. For most students, if something is *not* going to be assessed a clear message is received that it is not worth them spending time to learn it. When the assessment criteria are clear and precise, there is the danger that students will *only* learn what they need to guarantee their success in the assessment of their studies. It is therefore important to link assessment very strongly to intended learning outcomes so that, in one way or another, *all* the important learning outcomes are covered by assessment. It is equally vital not to overburden students with assessment (and also not to overburden tutors with marking). The quality of assessment is much more important than the quantity. This chapter brings together a number of factors, which can contribute to helping assessment to become an engine which drives open learning in the right directions and at sensible speeds.

The first three sets of suggestions in this chapter are about assessment by human beings: tutors. These are followed by three sets about computer-delivered assessment. Clearly, it is important to make the most of both kinds of assessment. Tutor time is far too valuable to waste on things which could just as well have been covered by a computer-marked assignment, or a computer-delivered exam. Human expertise and judgement needs to be reserved for those aspects of assessment which really do need human qualities, and tailored, responsive feedback to open learners individual work.

Any assessment process tends to favour those candidates who happen to be competent at handling it. For example, time constrained unseen written exams repeatedly reward students who happen to be good at preparing for, and coping with, time constrained unseen written exams. Similarly, computer-based assessment approaches favour candidates who are good at preparing for and undertaking such assessment. Diversifying assessment is needed to allow *all* learners the chance to display their full potential, without being unduly limited by what happens to be measured by just one or two favoured assessment formats. I offer some suggestions about ways of approaching the task of diversifying assessment for open learners.

I end this chapter by looking at assessment from another point of view, this time assessing the quality and effectiveness of the operation of an open learning pathway. Many of the criteria and principles have already been discussed in earlier parts of this book, but I end the book by bringing some of these together in the context of *learning from* the evaluation of open learning provision, as a means to adjusting it so that it will be even more effective the next time round.

# 44

# Designing tutor-marked assignments

However good a learning package is, we can only be sure that learners have succeeded if there is some tangible measure of their progress. Self-assessment questions can provide learners with a lot of practice, and can give them feedback, but it takes tutor-marked assignments to provide solid evidence of their progress *and* give them individual feedback. Designing effective tutor-marked assignments is one of the most significant parts of putting together an open learning programme. The following suggestions should help you to avoid many of the potential problems that can be associated with tutor-marked assignments.

1 **Look carefully at the intended learning outcomes.** Each question or task in tutor-marked assignments should be directly related to these outcomes. If it is found that an ideal tutor-marked assignment task goes beyond the stated learning outcomes, it is a strong signal to extend the published outcomes accordingly.

2 **Look carefully at the tasks where learners have already received feedback through self-assessment question responses.** It should be possible to avoid replicating the same tasks, unless it is really necessary for tutors to check that learners have indeed successfully mastered them.

3 **Use tutor-marked assignments to make best possible use of human feedback.** Tutor-marked assignments are best used when human judgement is needed, and when learners are likely to need more than the right answer or a good model answer to help them to make sense of how good (or how bad) their own attempts at an assignment are.

4 **Use tutor-marked assignments for things where it is usually necessary to talk through with face-to-face learners.** Most tutors or trainers who run live sessions know of those things which they often seem to need to explain to students. In open learning programmes, or flexible learning

elements in college-based programmes, it is useful to make sure that such elements are handled successfully by learners, and tutor-marked assignments provide a way of checking that learners have indeed succeeded with such areas.

5   **Use tutor-marked assignments to define the standards inherent in the intended learning outcomes.** It is often only possible to judge the standard or level of a learning package by looking at how the intended learning outcomes are going to be measured. When learners studying the package will also face formal exams, the tutor-marked assignments should prepare them well for the level of the questions they will meet then.

6   **Take particular care with the wording of the questions.** In face-to-face work with students, there is the benefit of tone of voice, emphasis and even facial expression to clarify the meaning of tasks set to students. Students can also ask for clarification when necessary. Tutor-marked assignments for open learners need to be just as clear – exactly as they are read by learners.

7   **Try the questions out on face-to-face students if possible.** Tutor-marked assignments in open learning materials can cause open learners to stop in their tracks! This is much less likely if you have had the chance to check that typical students can handle them successfully, and that there are not any unnoticed snags inherent in the questions.

8   **Find out how long it takes typical students to do the tutor-marked assignments.** This can then be the basis of advice to open learners. Don't, however, be too specific when phrasing such advice. It is better to suggest a range, for example, 'This assignment is intended to take you between two and four hours, but not longer than this'.

9   **Show open learners how the marks will be allocated.** Show how many marks go with each collection of short questions, or how the marks will be spread out between component parts of longer questions. This helps learners to see how much emphasis to give to each part of the assignment, and helps them to avoid spending too long on relatively unimportant parts of the assignment.

10  **Don't print the tutor-marked assignment questions in the open learning package.** Tutor-marked assignments are likely to need to be modified or adjusted long before the learning materials themselves need to be changed. Furthermore, you may wish to change the tutor-marked questions once it is likely that answers to them become available to future open learners from past ones. It is best to have the tutor-marked elements in a separate booklet, which could be much less expensive to change than the whole package.

# 45

# Designing marking schemes for tutor-marked assignments

Good marking schemes are particularly important when several different tutors will be marking open learners' work on the same assignments. Students are particularly good at finding out whether one tutor marks more severely than another! The following suggestions should help you to ensure that your tutor-marking is done as fairly and evenly as possible.

1    **Look back at the intended learning outcomes that are covered by each tutor-marked assignment.** Try to allocate marks across the range of assignments, so that all of the important parts of the outcomes are directly linked to marks.

2    **Use marking schemes to save time in assessing open learners' work.** A good marking scheme helps to make it much quicker for tutors to assess assignments, by helping to make each mark awarding decision as objective as possible. This is much to be preferred than having to look back over the whole assignment and award a 'gut feeling' overall mark.

3    **Make the marking scheme for each assignment as transparent as possible.** Ideally, *anyone* should be able to mark a particular example of an assignment, and give it just about the same mark using the marking scheme. This is best achieved by having each mark associated with something that should be clearly identifiable in each answer to the assignment.

4    **Strive to make the assessment valid.** This is about awarding marks for exactly what is deemed to be evidence of achievement of the particular learning outcomes involved. Be careful not to allow marks to be significantly affected by other matters arising in the assignment. For example, though it is tempting to dock marks for inadequacies in spelling, presentation, layout and so on, it is only *valid* to do so if such things are included in the intended outcomes. When something additional to the

original outcomes is felt to be important, it is worth either revising the outcomes, or making it clear to the open learners that so many marks will be allocated to identified additional aspects of their answers.

5 **Base the marking scheme on learners' answers.** It is not enough to design a marking scheme solely on what you *hope* learners will do with the assignment questions. Even with clearly worded questions, there will usually be some answers that you would not have expected, or some different ways of interpreting the question, which can still be perfectly valid.

6 **Consider linking the marking scheme to one or more model answers.** These should illustrate how *full marks* could be achieved for the assignment. Such answers may not be perfect, but should illustrate all that could be *reasonably* expected from learners studying the particular package concerned, at the level concerned.

7 **Use marking schemes to help open learners to see exactly what is really important.** The different marks allocated to each element of an answer to a question represent one of the most effective ways of helping learners to see what really counts. When they can see, for example, exactly what lost them various marks in their answers, they are much more likely not to repeat the same things in future work.

8 **Test out each marking scheme.** It is only possible to be sure that a marking scheme really works when several markers are seen to agree when applying the scheme to a sample of answers to the assignment. In practice, such trials lead to significant adjustments to the first design of the marking scheme, and often to some fine tuning of the wording of the question.

9 **Get tutors to practise with marking schemes in tutor training events.** This is clearly important for new tutors, but it is also useful to get experienced tutors to practise when introducing new assignments and new marking schemes. Aim to make marking schemes serve as a useful agenda on which tutors can base their feedback comments to learners on their work.

10 **Consider asking learners to self-assess their own work using the marking scheme.** Their work can still be given to tutors to mark. Tutors can then check whether the self-assessment was sufficiently objective, and can give feedback on areas of difficulty, both regarding misunderstandings that are evident through the self-assessment, and through the actual answers to the assignment questions. Getting open learners to do such self-assessment opens up the possibility of a tutor–learner dialogue about the assignment, and significantly deepens learners' experience of their attempts at the assignment itself.

# 46

# Monitoring the quality of tutor assessment

In colleges open learning tutoring of students studying flexible learning elements may be done by full-time or part-time employees of the institution. Then it would be quite normal for there to be various checks on the quality of the tutoring. When open learners are tutored by part-time staff, whose main job is for another institution (for example, university lecturers tutoring for the Open University), it is necessary to ensure that the quality of assessment and feedback is acceptable. The following suggestions may help you to decide how to approach setting up systems to monitor tutor performance.

1   **Appoint the right tutors in the first place.** There are many reasons why tutors might get into open learning support, ranging from a keen interest to find out about supporting learners working on their own or at a distance, to more pragmatic reasons such as to earn a little extra money. One indicator that high quality tutor support may be provided is a tutor's willingness to be trained and monitored. Where would-be tutors can furnish evidence that they have participated successfully in open learning tutoring already, check whether referees can comment on the quality of this aspect of their work.

2   **Build in appropriate filters in tutor-training.** While it is not possible to make an early diagnosis of every potential problem, people who are not going to turn out to be effective tutors to open learners often show this during training exercises on giving written feedback to open learners, or role-playing face-to-face or telephone encounters with students.

3   **Have some sort of record of each important encounter between tutors and learners.** For example, using triplicate forms for tutor-student feedback enables tutors to keep details of the main points they raised for each tutor-marked assignment, and provides a copy to be kept centrally. This allows the monitoring of tone, style and fairness, both on a continuous basis and retrospectively, when necessary.

4    **Arrange meetings between tutors.** Experienced open learning tutors can share a great deal about best practice with newer tutors. Such meetings can give tutors a realistic picture of the level of work expected from them, the amount of support they may be required to give, and how quickly they should aim to turn assignments round.

5    **Have double marking to check for consistency.** While it would be impossible (however desirable) to have all assignments double marked, it is usually possible to arrange that a representative sample of each tutor's assessments are remarked. This helps to fine tune standard setting.

6    **Monitor the drop out rate.** This can give important information about which tutors are providing the best support. It is, however, the least satisfactory way of monitoring tutor performance, as it can turn out to be based on things having gone seriously wrong before detection.

7    **Have systems whereby open learners can change their tutors.** Even with the best of tutors, there are occasionally differences of personality, style or approach that make them less than compatible with the occasional open learner. It is useful if there is an escape route for either party. It is even better if there is no enquiry or allocation of blame for the occasional request to switch. If a particular tutor is involved in such changes too often, then it is time to explore why.

8    **Ask open learners anonymously about the support they receive from their tutors.** This can conveniently be done by using computer-based multiple-choice questionnaires, or hand-written questionnaires. This sort of feedback is best analysed in terms of seeking general problems or directions for improvement, rather than as a prelude to trouble shooting matters arising in the work of individual tutors.

9    **Survey open learners' reactions to open-ended questions about the support they receive from their tutors.** This can, of course, be done 'behind tutors' backs', but is more productive if done through the tutors themselves, who can then also learn at first hand about the issues that they may wish to focus their attention on in the future development of their tutoring. Such surveying is best done *after* the open learners concerned have finished the module or unit concerned, so there are no tensions between feedback and assessment.

10   **Recognize and celebrate best practice.** Tutors who are performing well need to have confirmation that what they are doing is appreciated, and not just from their students. Write up illustrations of good practice, if necessary using anonymous names, in (for example) newsletters to tutors.

# 47

# Designing computer-marked assignments

Computer-marked assignments can save human toil, and can be a means of giving much quicker feedback to open learners than from human tutors. The following suggestions may help you to decide when and how to use computer-marked assignments.

1   **Look at examples from a range of sources.** There are many examples of structured questions in published computer-marked assignments and on the Internet. Seeing what other people have already done is the fastest way of working out what sorts of questions you could design for your own purposes.

2   **Decide whether you are designing *computer-delivered* assignments, or just *computer-marked* ones.** Computer-marked assignments can be in print with, for example, optical card-readers used to automate the marking, the print-out of feedback to learners, and the analysis of their scores and of the performance of the questions as testing devices. *Computer-delivered* assignments are where learners enter their answers or choices directly into a computer or terminal, and may then get feedback and/or scores straightaway from the machine, or across the Internet or an Intranet.

3   **Don't become trapped into the belief that computer-marked assignments can only test lower cognitive knowledge.** Although such assignments are often used to test straightforward recall of information or simple decision-making, well-designed assignments can test at a much deeper level. Look at the different things that can be tested, and the different question structures that are possible. Besides multiple-choice questions, computer-delivered assignments can be designed to use number-entry, text-entry, ranking, and a variety of other ways for learners to enter their answers or decisions.

4    **Decide which learning outcomes will be covered by the computer-aided assignment.** This is best done by working out which outcomes lend themselves best to testing using the range of formats available to you. Tell your open learners about this decision, so they are well informed about the content that they should prepare for the assignment.

5    **Think about computer literacy implications.** If the assignment is print-based, and only the *marking* is to be done using computers, there is little to worry about, other than to make sure that the instructions regarding how to fill in the optically readable card or sheet are clear and straight-forward. If, however, doing the assignment depends on sitting at a computer or terminal and interacting with it, open learners with highly developed keyboarding skills may be advantaged, as may those who have no fear of working with computers.

6    **Decide whether your use of computer-marked assignments will be summative or formative.** Technology can be used for both purposes, and even if you decide that your primary purpose is to measure your learners' achievement, you can still make use of the power of the technology to deliver feedback to your open learners.

7    **Explore the software options open to you.** There are several different software shells which support testing and feedback-delivery. Which you choose will depend on how sophisticated your question design will be, and to some extent how easily you yourself can learn to handle the software. Alternatively, your responsibility may rest mainly in the area of designing questions and feedback, with someone else handling the task of entering your assignments into the software.

8    **Try out each question thoroughly before including it in an assignment.** You may be able to test out your questions with face-to-face groups of students, giving you a great deal of useful feedback about whether your questions are really testing them, and which questions are too hard or too easy. Alternatively, you may be able to trial your questions in computer-based form as a part of learning materials, and get the software to analyse how each question performs. This helps you to make a better informed decision about which questions are good enough to include in a computer-marked assignment.

9   **Think about the security implications of assignments.** Where computer-delivered assignments count towards the overall assessment of open learners, ways may need to be found to prevent the correct answers from circulating around! Such ways include getting the cohort of learners together at the same time, and maybe in the same room, and doing the assignment in a way similar to a timed exam. Alternatively, ways may be found to keep learners, who have already done the exam, demonstrably separated from those who have not yet done it. A further option is delaying any feedback or information on scores until all learners have taken the test.

10  **Triangulate the results of computer-marked assignments.** At least until you know that a computer-marked assignment is performing reliably, and giving data that is consistent with *other* means of measuring your open learners' achievement, it is best to ensure that there are sufficient checks in the overall assessment system to find any snags with the computer-marked components. Be aware of the possibilities of some learners being so apprehensive of computers that their performance is not representative of their achievement. Also beware of substitution, for example, someone else doing the computer-marked component!

# 48

# Designing computer-generated feedback to open learners

We have already looked at the principles of designing feedback for open learners, both as a key part of responding to self-assessment questions, and responding to multiple-choice questions, whether used primarily for testing or for feedback. The following suggestions aim to help you to make computer-generated feedback as useful as possible to your learners.

1   **Don't miss out on the opportunity to couple feedback with assessment.** Whether you are using computer-marked assignments or computer-delivered exams, the technology makes it possible to give each open learner feedback on each choice of option or each keyed-in answer.

2   **Consider the pros and cons of instant feedback.** With computer-delivered exams, for example, it is possible for feedback to be given to learners immediately after they have attempted each question. The positive feedback they gain when they answer questions successfully may boost their morale and lead to improved exam performance, but the opposite may happen if they happen to get the first few questions wrong.

3   **Consider 'slightly delayed' feedback.** It is useful if learners can receive feedback while they still remember what they were thinking of when they answered the questions. In computer-delivered exams, feedback can be shown to learners on-screen *after* they have completed all of the questions, and when it will not have any effect on their scores.

4   **Think how best to give feedback if it is delayed more significantly.** For example, when sending computer-generated feedback print-outs to open learners in response to their computer-marked assignments, there will

normally be at least several days between learners answering the questions and receiving feedback. It is then necessary to make sure that learners are reminded of the context in which they answered each question.

5    **Always remind learners both of the question and of the options from which they have selected.** It is important, for example in multiple-choice formats, not only to remind open learners about the context surrounding the correct (or best) option, but also to remind them of the options which were wrong (or less good).

6    **Use technology to write letters to learners.** Particularly with computer-marked assignments, it is relatively straightforward to wrap up the feedback printed out for each question into a self-sufficient letter, commenting additionally on their overall performance.

7    **Letters can be written for computer-delivered exams too.** It is possible for learners doing a computer-delivered exam, in a formal examination room, to leave the room at the end of the exam and pick up a personal letter informing them not only of their overall performance, but also giving feedback where appropriate on each question they have attempted. Getting exam feedback so quickly, and in a form where it can be reread, is a powerful way of preventing this kind of formal examination from being a lost learning opportunity.

8    **Start the feedback on a personal note.** Computers can be programmed to start a letter with 'Dear Alison' rather than 'Dear Mrs Jones'. Most open learners prefer the personal touch, especially when the feedback is coming from a machine. It is, however, important to use familiar names only if you know what your learners prefer to be called. The start of the letter can then give one of two or three 'openings', each designed for learners who have respectively scored brilliantly, average or not so well.

9    **End the feedback letter with useful advice.** The computer can be programmed to search for topic areas where learners' answers have shown particular strengths or weaknesses, and can offer topic-specific praise or suggestions. It is also useful to end a computer-delivered assignment feedback letter with something useful regarding preparation for the next assignment on the programme.

10   **Don't make computer-generated feedback anonymous!** When the name of the tutor who designed the assignment is printed at the end of computer-generated feedback letters, this person is likely to receive quite a few communications from open learners (even if the name used was a fictitious one!) If the tone of each feedback response is warm and helpful, open learners do not feel that the feedback was dreamt up by a machine.

# 49

# Designing multiple-choice exams

When multiple-choice questions are used for exams rather than just for self-assessment, feedback or diagnostic testing, much more care needs to be taken regarding the design and validation of the questions. The following suggestions may help you to devise effective multiple-choice exams.

1   **Check the performance of each question with large numbers of students before including it in an exam.** The most suitable questions are those which discriminate between the able and less able candidates. There are statistical packages which can help you work out the 'facility-value' of questions (how easy or difficult they are), and the 'discrimination index' of questions (how well they separate the best candidates from the rest). Ideally, all questions should have been through trialling with hundreds of students before using the questions in a formal exam. An advantage of multiple-choice exams is that it is perfectly possible to arrange for students to get not only their scores very quickly, but also detailed feedback reminding them of their correct decisions, and explaining why other decisions were incorrect.

2   **Make sure that candidates aren't going to be getting questions right for the wrong reasons.** Look for any give-aways in the keys or context of the questions. During trialling, if too many learners get a question right, it could be that the question is too easy to serve a useful purpose in testing, or it is sometimes the case that something is giving away the correct option to choose.

3    **Watch out for cases where the best candidates choose a distractor.** This usually happens when they can see something wrong with the option which is supposed to be undeniably correct, or 'best'. This can be done manually, by scanning the responses from a large group of students, and with prior knowledge of who the most able students are. Computer software can normally help by identifying all learners who have got a particular question wrong, and can be programmed to search for candidates with a high overall score who get these particular questions wrong.

4    **Start the exam with some relatively straightforward questions.** This helps anxious candidates to get into their stride, and is better than having such candidates thrown into a panic by an early tricky question.

5    **Help candidates to develop their skills at tackling multiple-choice exams.** Give candidates past papers to practise on, and provide advice on the most effective techniques for tackling this form of exam.

6    **Get the timing right.** Decide whether you really want an against-the-clock exam. Find out how long candidates take on average. With a timed exam, there is some tendency for candidates to rush their decision making, and even if they have plenty of time left over, they are still left with a hangover legacy of questions where they made wrong decisions.

7    **Look for ways of making marking quick and easy.** When large numbers of candidates are involved, it is worth looking at optical mark reading techniques or computer-aided testing formats.

8    **Get some colleagues to take your exam.** They may be surprised at things they find that they did not know, and they may give you some surprises too about what you *thought* were cut-and-dried questions.

9    **Form a regional network.** Teaming up with other colleagues in your discipline, who are also developing multiple-choice testing, can lead towards building up a good bank of tried and tested questions.

10   **Arrange for quick feedback to learners, if possible.** If your exam is computer-generated, it can be designed to produce a score at any time, either when students have finished it, or as a running total. Students can also be given feedback on their choices either on-screen as they work through the test, or on-screen after they have finished, or as a printout when they leave the exam room.

# 50

# Diversifying the assessment of open learners

All forms of assessment, in open learning and in education and training in general, can be said to disadvantage some learners. For example, unseen written exams favour candidates who happen to be skilled at preparing for and sitting such exams, and so on. The following suggestions aim to help you to allow all of your open learners the opportunity to show their potential at its best in at least some of the assessment formats they encounter.

1   **Remind yourself of why learners are being assessed.** Is it to measure their performance overall? Is it to certify their achievement in particular areas of competence? Are the learning outcomes associated with their open learning being assessed alongside other outcomes that they covered in class-based situations? The reasons for assessing your learners should inform the choices of the forms in which they are assessed.

2   **Look again at each intended learning outcome.** Ask yourself 'what is the most appropriate way to measure achievement of this?' Check that what is being assessed is not just the ability of learners to *write* about something that they have understood, nor just their ability to *make decisions* about a particular cross-section of what they have learnt. To be valid, the overall assessment should aim as far as possible to measure how well your learners have achieved each of the intended outcomes.

3   **Try to triangulate assessment.** Especially with important learning outcomes, look for more than one way of measuring them. This can help to find those open learners who may have achieved the outcome concerned, but whose assessment technique may let them down in one form of assessment, but who demonstrate their achievement much more successfully with another form. Maybe in such circumstances, it should be the best performance which is included in the overall assessment.

4    **Don't measure the same skills over and over again.** For example, marked essays and reports tend to favour candidates who are skilled at performing well in these formats, and who write purposeful introductions, coherent 'middles' and robust conclusions. While these skills are useful, it is not desirable to reward them time and time again. Use such assessment formats sparingly, and measure these skills well, but not repeatedly.

5    **Look at the advantages of short-form assignments.** For example, getting open learners to write an essay plan instead of an essay, or a short-form report instead of a full one, can cause them to do almost as much thinking as they would have done for a full essay or report. The essay plans or short-form reports are much less of a burden to assess, and can be assessed at least as objectively as would have been the case with the longer alternatives.

6    **Involve open learners in applying assessment criteria.** Give your learners opportunities to 'mark' past examples of essays, assignments, reports, and so on. This can alert them to successful practice – and things to avoid! More importantly, getting learners to use assessment criteria lets them in on the assessment culture in which they are working, and helps them see what will be looked for in their own work in due course.

7    **Consider coupling self-assessment with tutor-marked or computer-marked assignments.** Most assessment forms play their part in driving learning, but this is a way to make at least some assessments enhance learning too. For example, asking open learners to complete a self-assessment pro forma along with assignments sent in for tutor-marking, helps to ensure that learners derive additional learning payoff, both from their reflections on their work before marking and from feedback from tutors *about* their self-assessment. While it can be argued that some assessments are intended to be summative, and that feedback is not the real agenda in such cases, it is still possible to build some self-assessment into such assignments.

8    **Look for alternative ways in which open learners can demonstrate the success of their learning.** There are numerous alternatives to written essays or reports. These include posters, portfolios of evidence, and presentations given by learners to groups of their peers (which is possible, for example, when open learning pathways are being used in college-based courses). Each different alternative allows some learners the opportunity to show their achievements in ways that may be more comfortable (and more successful) than they would have been in, say, formal exams or traditionally assessed coursework.

9    **Consider the part that can be played by electronic communication.** Tutor-marked assignments can be sent electronically, and an increasing proportion of open learners find working on computers preferable to picking up pen and paper. Feedback can be returned to them by e-mail too, including marking up their work with feedback comments and sending it back to them. This can work equally well as a means of assessing learners at a distance, or students studying flexible learning elements in college-based courses. In either case, time and some costs (for example paper, postage, and administration) can be saved by using technology, where such technology is already available to learners.

10   **Consider peer-assessment possibilities.** Even if peer-assessment does not count significantly in the context of the overall assessment framework, the amount of feedback that open learners can give each other (face-to-face or using electronic communication) is well worth the time spent setting up peer-assessment opportunities. Looking at someone else's attempt at an assignment can often teach open learners even more about their own attempt than they may have gained from direct feedback from a tutor.

# 51

# Piloting and adjusting open learning materials

A great deal is usually learnt during the first run with a new open learning package. The same applies to the use of study guides to support and direct students' learning from traditional resource materials. The following suggestions may help you to make piloting a central plank of the quality assurance of your open learning provision.

1  **Pilot at the earliest possible stage.** Don't wait until the materials have been professionally produced. Try to get some learners to work through the materials even when they are in draft form. Gather as much feedback as you can, so that you can edit and polish the materials before producing them in any significant quantities. Binning large quantities of unsatisfactory first editions is expensive as well as frustrating!

2  **Use questionnaires to collect some of your feedback from open learners.** Make the questionnaires short enough to guarantee a good response rate. If necessary, build in some sort of incentive to make sure everyone responds – prize draws have been used. An alternative is to include the feedback questionnaire in an assessed task (but not necessarily to try to link marks to the worth of the feedback).

3  **Include some open-ended questions.** One of the problems with structured questionnaires is that you only get the answers to the questions you have asked. With open-ended questions, your learners have the chance to tell you about other issues or problems that they feel you should know. Useful questions can be as simple as, 'What were the two things you liked best about working through this package?' and, 'What do you think is the most important change that should be made in the next edition?'

4   **Gather at least some feedback using structured interviews with learners.** Ask them what they had in mind when they provided earlier written feedback. Allow them to explain what they really meant to say. Make it clear that you welcome critical feedback and that you are prepared to act on it.

5   **Use all further data that gives you feedback.** Tutor-marked assignment performance is often an early indicator of strengths and weaknesses in open learning materials. Learners' subsequent performance in examinations often gives additional information about which parts of the open learning materials worked effectively and helped them to achieve the intended outcomes.

6   **Start adjusting the materials as soon as feedback becomes available.** For example, write in suggested changes on a master-copy of the materials, using a different colour to make your planned changes easy to see, and dating each change, so that you can see later on how the feedback information emerged.

7   **Adjust tutor-marked assignment questions first.** It is usually these parts of open learning materials (or study guides), where changes are most urgent. The first few answers from students often show unanticipated problems, many of which can be averted by adjusting the wording of the questions or briefings.

8   **Adjust self-assessment questions and feedback responses.** Whether in self-standing open learning materials, computer-based packages or in study guides, the self-assessment elements are usually the most significant parts to adjust as you gain a picture about the problems or difficulties learners experience. It is often worth adding further self-assessment elements designed to counter such problems.

9   **Look for sudden jumps in the materials.** Ask learners to identify any stages where they became stuck, or where an argument unfolded in a way that they could not follow. Such difficulties are often remedied by only a sentence or two of additional explanation, inserted at the most suitable point in the materials.

10  **Where necessary, modify the wording and level of learning outcomes.** The need for such changes often becomes evident when piloting materials. For example, if learners are obviously spending too much time on a particular element of their studies, and learning it too well compared to other more important elements, changes in the ways that the respective learning outcomes are expressed can be helpful.

# Appendix 1   A quality checklist for flexible learning materials

The following checklist is presented as a summary of many of the main points I have made in this book. It is adapted from criteria I first published in *The Open Learning Handbook* (1994) and *The Lecturer's Toolkit* (1998). The checklist is particularly intended to help you to make decisions about the strengths and weaknesses of published resource materials, but may well be useful as a framework to address the quality of materials you design yourself. The questions are clustered as follows:

- Objectives or statements of intended learning outcomes
- Structure and layout
- Self-assessment questions and activities (learning by doing)
- Responses to self-assessment questions and activities (feedback)
- Introductions, summaries and reviews
- The text itself
- Diagrams, charts, tables, graphs, and so on
- Some general points

## Objectives or statements of intended learning outcomes

1   **Is there a clear indication of any prerequisite knowledge or skills?** If not, you may usefully compose a specification of what is being taken for granted regarding the starting point of the materials. It is particularly important, that when flexible learning elements are being used within college-based traditional courses, students should know where the flexible learning outcomes fit into the overall picture of their courses.

2 **Are the objectives stated clearly and unambiguously?** This is where you may wish to 'translate' the objectives of particular learning packages, making them more directly relevant to the students who will use them. This can often be done by adding 'for example,' illustrations of how and when the intended outcomes will be relevant to their own situations.

3 **Are the objectives presented in a meaningful and 'friendly' way?** (ie, *not* 'the expected learning outcomes of this module are that the student will...'). I suggest that it is preferable to write learning outcomes using language such as, 'When you've worked through Section 3, you'll be able to...' It is important that students develop a sense of ownership of the intended learning outcomes, and it is worthwhile making sure that the outcomes as presented to them make them feel involved, and that the expressed outcomes do not just belong to the learning package.

4 **Do the objectives avoid 'jargon' which may not be known to students before starting the material?** It is, of course, normal for new terms and concepts to be introduced in any kind of learning, but it is best if this is done in ways that avoid frightening off students at the outset. It may remain necessary to include unfamiliar words in the objectives of a learning package, but this can still allow for such words to be explained there and then legitimising a starting point of 'not yet knowing' such words. Adding a few words in brackets along the lines of, 'this means in practice that...' can be a useful way ahead in such cases.

## Structure and layout

5 **Is the material visually attractive, thereby helping students to want to learn from it?** It is not always possible to choose the materials that *look* best, however. Sometimes the best looking materials may be too expensive, or they may not be sufficiently relevant to learning needs. At the end of the day, it is the materials that *work* best that are cost-effective, so compromises may have to be made on visual attractiveness.

6 **Is there sufficient white space?** In print-based materials this is needed for students to write their own notes on, answer questions posed by the materials, do calculations and exercises, which help them make sense of the ideas they have been reading about, and so on. A learning package which allows – or insists on – students writing all over it, is likely to be more effective at promoting effective learning by doing.

7     **Is it easy for students to find their way backwards and forwards?** This is sometimes called 'signposting' and includes good use of headings in print-based materials, or effective menus in computer-based materials. Either way, well-signposted materials allow students to get quickly to anything they want to consolidate (or 'digest'), as well as helping them to scan ahead to get the feel of what is to come.

8     **Is the material broken into manageable chunks?** Students' concentration spans are finite. We all know how fickle concentration is at face-to-face training sessions. The same applies when students are learning from resource materials. If an important topic goes on for page after page, we should not be surprised if concentration is lost. Frequent headings, subheadings, tasks and activities can all help to avoid students falling into a state of limbo when working through learning packages.

9     **Does the material avoid any sudden jumps in level?** A sudden jump can be a 'shut the package' cue to students working on their own. It is just about impossible for authors of learning materials to tell when they have gone one step too far, too fast. The first people to discover such sudden jumps are always the students who cannot understand why the material has suddenly left them floundering. In well-piloted materials, such difficulties will have been ironed out long before the packages reach their published forms, but not all materials have waited for this vital process to happen.

## Self-assessment questions and activities (learning by doing)

10    **Are there plenty of them?** For example, I suggest that there should be one in sight per double page spread in print-based materials, or something to do on most screens in interactive computer-based packages. If we accept that learning mostly happens by practising, making decisions, or having a go at exercises, it is only natural that effective interactive learning materials are essentially packaged up learning by doing.

11    **Are the tasks set by the questions clear and unambiguous?** In live sessions, if a task is not clear to students, someone will ask about it, and clarification will follow. With packaged learning resources, it is crucial to make sure that people working on their own do not have to waste time and energy working out exactly what the instructions mean every time they come to some learning by doing.

12 **Are the questions and tasks inviting?** Is it clear to students that it is valuable for them to have a go rather than skip the tasks or activities? It is sometimes an art to make tasks so interesting that no one is tempted to give them a miss, especially if they are quite difficult ones. However, it helps if you can make the tasks as relevant as possible to students' own backgrounds and experiences.

13 **Is there enough space for students to write their answers?** In print-based materials, it is important to get students writing. If they just *think* about writing something, but don't *do* it, they may well forget what they might have written! In computer-based materials, it is equally important to ensure that users make decisions, for example by choosing an option in a multiple-choice exercise, so that they can then receive feedback directly relating to what they have just done.

14 **Collectively, do the self-assessment questions and activities test students' achievement of the objectives, and prepare them for any final assessments they may be heading towards?** Perhaps one of the most significant dangers of resource-based learning materials is that it is often easier to design tasks and exercises on unimportant topics, than it is to ensure that students' activities focus on the things that are involved in them achieving the intended learning outcomes. To eliminate this danger, it is useful to check that each and every intended learning outcome is cross-linking to one or more self-assessment questions or activities, so that students get practice in everything that is important. The self-assessment questions should collectively prepare students for any other assessments that they will experience after completing their open learning.

# Responses to self-assessment questions and activities (feedback)

15 **Are they really responses to what students will have done?** (ie, not just answers to the questions). We saw earlier in this chapter how important it is for students to get the chance to learn through feedback on their efforts. If someone cannot get the correct answer to a question, telling them the answer is of very limited value. They need feedback on what was wrong with their own attempt at answering the question. In face-to-face training, they can get such responses from their lecturer. In resource-based learning, such feedback needs to be available to them in predetermined ways, in print or in feedback responses which appear on their computer screens.

16    **Do the responses meet each student's need to find out:**
      *'Was I right?'*
      *'If not, why not?'*
      When students get a self-assessment question or activity 'right', it is quite
      straightforward to provide them with appropriate feedback. It is when
      they get them wrong that they need all the help we can give them. In
      particular, they need not only to know what the correct answer should
      have been, but also what was wrong with their own answers. Multiple-
      choice question formats are particularly useful here, as they allow different
      students making different mistakes each to receive individual feedback
      on their own attempts at such questions.

17    **Do the responses include encouragement or affirmation (without being
      patronising) for students who got them right?** It is easy enough to start
      a response with words such as 'well done'. However, there are many
      different ways of giving praise, and saying 'splendid' may be fine if the
      task was difficult and we really want to reward students who got it right,
      but the same 'splendid' can come across as patronising if students felt
      that it was an easy question.

18    **Do the responses include something that will help students who got it
      wrong *not* to feel like complete idiots?** Do the responses give them
      guidance on what an acceptable answer might look like? One of the
      problems of working alone with resource-based learning materials is that
      people who get things wrong may feel they are the only people ever to
      have made such mistakes. When a difficult question or task is likely to
      cause students to make mistakes or to pick incorrect options, it helps them
      a lot if there are some words of comfort such as, 'this was a tough one!' or,
      'most people get this wrong at first'.

## Introductions, summaries and reviews

19    **Is each part introduced in an interesting, stimulating way?** There is no
      second chance to make a good first impression! If students are put off a
      topic by the way it starts, they may never recover that vital 'want' to
      learn it.

20    **Do the introductions alert students to the way the materials are designed
      to work?** Learning resource materials should not assume that all students
      have developed the kinds of study skills needed for flexible learning. It is
      best when the authors of such materials share with students the way that
      they intend the optimum learning payoff to be achieved. When students
      know where they are intended to be going, there is more chance they will
      get there.

21  **Are there clear and useful summaries or reviews?** Do these help students to digest what they have learnt? In any good face-to-face session, lecturers take care to cover the main points more than once, and to remind students towards the end of the session about the most important things they should remember. When designing learning resource materials, authors sometimes think that it is enough to put across the main points well – and only once! Summaries and reviews are every bit as essential in good learning materials as they are in live sessions.

22  **Do summaries and reviews provide useful ways for students to revise the material quickly and effectively?** A summary or review helps students to identify the essential learning points they should have mastered. Once they have done this, it should not take much to help them retain such mastery, and they may well not need to work through the whole package ever again if they can polish their grasp of the subject just by reading summaries or reviews.

## The text itself

23  **Is it readable, fluent and unambiguous?** When students are working on their own, there is no one to ask if something is not clear. Good learning resource materials depend a lot on the messages getting across. Those people who never use a short word when they can think of a longer alternative, should not be allowed to create learning resource materials! Similarly, short sentences tend to get messages across more effectively than longer sentences.

24  **Is it relevant?** For example, does the material keep to the objectives as stated, and do these fit comfortably into the overall picture of the course or module? It can be all too easy for the creators of learning resource materials to get carried away with their pet subjects, and go into far more detail than is reasonable.

25  **Is the tone 'involving' where possible?** Is there plenty of use of 'you' for the student, 'I' for the author, 'we' for the student and author together? This is a matter of style. Some writers find it hard to communicate in an informal, friendly manner. There is plenty of evidence that communication works best in learning materials when students feel involved, and feel that the learning package is 'talking' to them in a natural and relaxed way.

# Diagrams, charts, tables, graphs, and so on

26 **Is each non-text component as self-explanatory as possible?** In face-to-face training sessions, there are all sorts of clues as to what any illustrations (for example, overheads or slides) actually mean. Lecturers' tone-of-voice and facial expressions do much to add to the explanation, as well as the words they use when explaining directly. With learning packages, it is important that such explanation is provided when necessary in print.

27 **Do the students know what to do with each illustration?** They need to know whether they need to learn it, label or complete it, to note it in passing, or to pick out the trend, or even nothing. In a face-to-face session, when lecturers show, for example, a table of data, someone is likely to ask, 'Do we have to remember these figures?' If the same table of data is included in learning materials, the same question still applies, but there is no one to reply to it. Therefore, good learning resource materials need to anticipate all such questions, and clarify to students exactly what the expectations are regarding diagrams, charts and so on. It only takes a few words of explanation to do this, along such lines as, 'you don't have to remember these figures, but you do need to be able to pick out the main trend' or, 'you don't have to be able to draw one of these, but you need to be able to recognize one when you see one'.

28 **'A sketch can be more useful than 1000 words': is the material sufficiently illustrated?** One of the problem areas with flexible learning materials is that they are sometimes written all-in-words, at the expense of visual ways of communicating important messages. Sometimes the explanation is simply that the writer of the materials is not confident about providing sketches or diagrams. However, good quality materials overcome this weakness, by using the services of someone with the appropriate talents.

# Some general points

29 **Does the material ensure that the average student will achieve the objectives?** This, of course, is one of the most important questions we can ask of any learning package. If the answer is 'no', it's probably worth looking for a better package.

30 **Will the average student *enjoy* using the material?** In some ways this is the ultimate question. When students 'can't put the package down, because it is so interesting to work through it' there is not usually much wrong with the package.

31    **How up to date is the material covered?** How quickly will it date? Will it have an adequate shelf life as a learning resource, and will the up-front costs of purchasing it or developing it be justified?

32    **How significant is the 'not invented here' syndrome?** Can you work with the differences between the approach used in the material and your own approach? Can you integrate comfortably and seamlessly the two approaches with your students? (If you criticize or put-down learning resource materials your students are using, you are quite likely to destroy their confidence in using the material, and their belief in the quality of the content of the material as a whole).

33    **How expensive is the material?** Can students realistically be expected to acquire their own copies of it? Can bulk discounts or shareware arrangements be made? If the material is computer-based, is it suitable for networking, and is this allowed within copyright arrangements?

34    **Can students reasonably be expected to gain sufficient access?** This is particularly crucial when large groups are involved. Could lack of access to essential resource materials be cited as grounds for appeal by students who may be unsuccessful when assessed on what is covered by the resource material? This particularly applies to information technology laboratories and personal computers, when they play an important part in flexible learning delivery. Are part-time students disproportionately disadvantaged in terms of information technology access?

35    **What alternative ways are there of students learning the topic concerned?** What complementary ways are there in which students can combine other ways of learning the topic with their learning from the resource material in question?

36    **How is the resource material or medium demonstrably better than the cheapest or simplest way of learning the topic?** There need to be convincing answers to this question, not least regarding expenditure.

37    **Will it make students' learning more efficient?** How will it save them time, or how will it focus their learning more constructively?

38    **Will the resource material or medium be equally useful to all students?** Will there be no instances of disadvantaging of, for example, students learning in a second language, women students, mature students, students who are not good with computers, and so on?

39    **What additional Key Skills outcomes will students derive from using the material?** Are these outcomes assessed? Could they outweigh the *intended* learning outcomes?

40    **How can feedback on the effectiveness of the resource material be sought?** What part should be played by peer-feedback from colleagues, feedback from student questionnaires, observations of students' reactions to the material and assessment of students' learning?

# Appendix 2   Extending self-assessment: an example

## Self-assessment and tutor-dialogue form

Please complete your part of each of the questions below as objectively as you can, and hand this form in with your assignment. The aims of this self-assessment are:

- to give you an opportunity to reflect on the work you are about to hand in;
- to give you further feedback on your work and on your own self-assessment of your work

Fill in the parts in bold; your tutor will respond where necessary after the *italics* prompts. Your comments on this form will not affect your assessment.

Your name: _____

Date: _____

Title of Assignment: _____

_____

*Tutor's name:*_____

*Date of marking:* _____

1 What do you honestly consider will be a fair score or grade for the work you are handing in?

Your estimate: Tutor's score/grade:

*Tutor's comments on agreement between your self-assessment and the tutor assessment scores or grades:*

2 What do you think was the thing you did best in this assignment?

*Tutor's reply on the above:*

3 If you had the chance to do the assignment again from scratch, how (if at all) might you decide to go about it differently?

*Tutor's reply to your second thoughts:*

4    What did you find the hardest aspect of this assignment?

*Tutor's comment on how you actually did on this aspect:*

5    List below up to three aspects of your work, which you would
     particularly like to have your tutor's opinions about.

Aspects:                          *Tutor's opinions:*

•                                 •

•                                 •

•                                 •

6    Please give details of any additional help or support, which you
     would have liked to help you to approach this assignment more
     effectively:

*Tutor's replies or comments:*

7    Please list up to three (short) questions you would like your tutor to answer in connection with the subject matter on which this assignment was based:

Your questions:                    *Tutor's replies:*

•                                  •

•                                  •

•                                  •

8    How difficult (5) or easy (1) did you find this assignment?

5...................4.......................3....................2....................1

9    Approximately how long did it take you to complete this assignment?

10    Any final comments from you:

11    *Any further replies or comments from your tutor:*

*Notes*: the pro forma above is designed to illustrate the principle only. In practice, it is much better to design a corresponding pro forma relating to the individual assignment about which the dialogue is to take place, with subject-specific questions as well as general ones. Otherwise, learners would soon become bored at answering exactly the same questions about successive assignments and the dialogue would be less productive. In any case, the pro forma should not become a burden either to students or to tutors, and I suggest should be limited to two sides of A4.

You may feel that the burden to tutors of replying to each of the learner's questions and comments could be intolerable. However, such a pro forma can be a useful short cut to provide tutor feedback to learners. For example, where learners already indicate on the form that they know what is wrong with their work as submitted, tutors do not need to spell out such details.

# Some further reading on open and flexible learning

There is a wide and rapidly expanding literature on open, flexible and distance learning, and on the closely related themes of computer-based learning, information technology and electronic communication. The sources selected below are only the tip of the iceberg, but may represent useful starting points for further exploration of some of the issues addressed in the present book.

Bates, A W (1995) *Technology, Open Learning and Distance Education* Routledge, London.

Black, D *et al* (1998) *500 Tips on Getting Published*, Kogan Page, London.

Bourner, T and Race, P (1995) *How to Win as a Part-Time Student (2nd Edition)* Kogan Page, London.

Daniel, J S (1996) *Mega-Universities and Knowledge Media: Technology Strategies for Higher Education* Kogan Page, London.

Edwards, R (1997) *Changing Places? Flexibility, Lifelong Learning and a Learning Society* Routledge, London.

Evans, T and Nation, D (1996) *Opening Education: Policies and Practices from Open and Distance Education* Routledge, London.

Gibbs, G (1994) (with various co-authors) *Course Design for Resource-Based Learning* Separate volumes covering respectively the following disciplines: *Social Science, Education, Technology, Accountancy, Built Environment, Art and Design, Business, Humanities, Science*: Oxford Centre for Staff and Learning Development, Oxford Brookes University, Oxford.

Laurillard, D (1993) *Rethinking University Teaching* Routledge, London.

Lockwood, F (ed.) (1995) *Open and Distance Learning Today* Routledge, London.

Mitchell, C (1997) *Transforming Teaching: selecting and evaluating teaching strategies* FEDA F.E. Matters, Vol.1 No.14, FEDA, Blagdon, Bristol, UK.

Race, P (1994) *The Open Learning Handbook (2nd edition)* Kogan Page, London.

Race, P and Brown, S (1998) *The Lecturer's Toolkit* Kogan Page, London.

Rowntree, D (1992) *Exploring Open and Distance Learning* Kogan Page, London.

Rowntree, D (1994) *Preparing Materials for Open, Distance and Flexible Learning* Kogan Page, London.

Wade, W *et al* (1994) *Flexible Learning in Higher Education* Kogan Page, London.

# Index

adapting learning materials   37–56
adopting learning materials   37–56
agenda setting   92
anxious learners   34
assessment   16, 21, 27, 66, 69, 72, 97, 123, 129, 136–53
assessment criteria   16, 152,
assessment: diversifying   151–3
assessment security   146
audio-conferencing   110
audiotape   86, 99–101

background material   28
benefits for colleges/training providers   25–7
benefits for employers/managers   22–4
benefits for learners/trainees   17–18, 127, 129
benefits for lecturers/trainers   19–21
briefings   52

collaborative learning   14, 130–32
college-based learning   25–7, 31–3, 48–50
comfort of privacy   85, 129
commentaries   55
communications technologies   94–116
competences   71–2
computer-assisted learning   9, 102–104
computer conferencing   108–110
computer-delivered assessment   33, 144–6
computer-generated feedback   147–8
computer-marked assignments   144–6
conclusions   89–90
content relevance   45–7
costing   44
curriculum selection   28–31, 68
cut-and-paste   56

delivery dates   51
diagrams   162

distance learning   7
distractors   80–81, 150
double marking   143

elements of competence   71
e-mail   105–107, 125
English, plain   68
entry levels   12
essays and essay plans   152
evidence descriptors   72

face-to-face   121, 130
feedback from learners   90, 104, 126, 143, 154–5
feedback to learners   10, 23, 29, 42, 55, 66, 74, 76–8, 82–3, 84–6, 92, 103, 106–107, 111, 122–3, 124–5, 138, 147–8, 150
flexibility   12–14
flexible learning   8

headings   67
high fliers   34

independent learning   8
individualised learning   8
information technologies   94–116
interactive learning   9, 33, 42, 55,
Internet   114–16
interviews   155
intranets   114
introductions   67, 87–8, 160

job security   21

key   79
large-group teaching   31–3,
layout   43, 157–8
learner profiles   59–61
learning blocks   35
learning-by-doing   10, 16, 22, 29, 46, 66, 103, 128, 158–9

learning organization   27
learning outcomes   16, 42, 45, 49, 52, 54, 66, 68–70, 74, 91, 96, 102–103, 115, 140, 151, 155, 156–7, 159
lectures   31–3
limitations   127
low fliers   34
lower cognitive knowledge   144

marking schemes   85, 140–41
media   11, 94–116
mentors   133–5
model answers   85, 141
motivation   111, 128
multimedia   111–13
multiple-choice   74, 79–81, 82–3, 149–150

National Vocational Qualifications (UK)   71
not-invented-here syndrome   41, 46, 163

open-ended tasks   75, 84–6
ownership   43

pace of learning   11, 13
part-time learners   35
peer-assessment   132, 153
performance criteria   72
personal copies   51
piloting   56, 70, 154–5
place of learning   11, 13
praise   77, 82, 90, 123
prerequisite knowledge/skills   11, 69, 156
profiles of open learners   59–61
published materials   42–7

questionnaires   154

range statements   72
remedial material   29
resource-based learning   5, 8, 15–16, 24
responses   42, 55, 66, 74, 76–8, 82–3, 84–6, 92, 159–60

retention   50
reviews   45, 89–90, 161

second language learning   35
self-assessment tutor dialogue   165–9
self-assessment questions   55, 73–5, 76–8, 79–83, 84–6, 91, 152, 158–9
sentence length   64, 70, 125
special needs   36
staff development   26
standards   23, 43, 139
start dates   12
stem   80
strategy for writing   65–7
student-centred learning   8
study guides   91–3
study-skills   53, 93, 127–29
summaries   89–90, 161
supported self-study   8
sympathy messages   77, 83

target audience   66
telephone feedback   125
timescales   46, 104
tone and style   43, 62–4, 161
tracking software   104
trialling   49, 145, 154–5
tutor-marked assignments   55, 84, 101, 117–135, 138–141, 152
tutor support   11, 13, 23, 117–135
tutor training   122–3, 142
tutors: monitoring   142–3

understanding   69

video   96–8
video-conferencing   110
virtual classrooms   108

wanting to learn   10
watching learning   49
white space   157
whole-group feedback   126
writing open learning materials   57–93